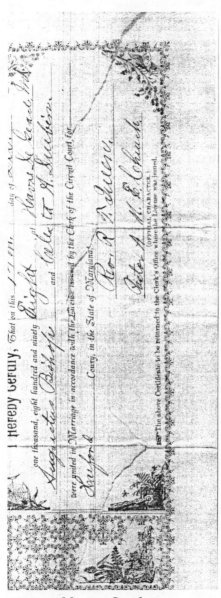

I Hereby Certify, That on this ___ day of ___

one thousand, eight hundred and ninety Eight ___ ___ ___

Augustus Bishop and Coletta A. Suiter ___

were united in Marriage in accordance with the License issued by the Clerk of the Circuit Court for

Harford ___ County, in the State of Maryland.

Rev. R. R. ___

Pastor M. E. Church

(OFFICIAL CHARACTER.)

☞ The above Certificate to be returned to the Clerk's Office where the License was issued.

Marriage Certificate

Know all men by these presents
that I Henry Barnes of Harford County
and State of Maryland for divers good and
sufficient considerations me thereunto moving
have released from slavery, manumitted and
set free and by these presents do hereby release from slavery, liberate manumit and
set free my negro man named Isaac Bishop
now aged forty one years, he being able to work
and gain a sufficient livelihood and maintenance and him the said negro Isaac Bishop
I do declare to be henceforth free, manumitted
and discharged from all manner of service or
servitude to me, my executors or administrators
forever —

In witness whereof I have hereunto
set my hand and affixed my seal on this
seventeenth day of November in the year of
Our Lord one thousand eight hundred and
fifty four —

                      Henry Barnes (seal)

Signed, sealed and de-
livered in the presence of us.
Wm Jarman J. P.
Henry S. Hugger

State of Maryland
          Harford County set
                         On this seventeenth
day of November eighteen hundred and fifty four
personally appeared Henry Barnes before me the
subscriber a justice of the peace of the state of
Maryland

Freedom Certificate

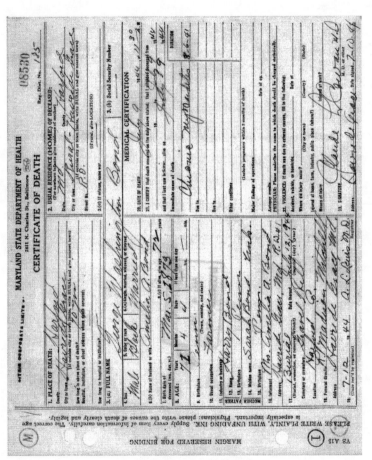

Death Certificate

"Those of us who've delighted in observing Reggie Bishop's infectious enthusiasm and hearing of his insight and adventures in genealogy are delighted that the country as a whole will now be able to read about a grown man being so carried away with his research that he got himself accidentally locked after hours in a courthouse basement."

Jim Chrismer
Publications Director
Historical Society of Harford County (MD)

"*The Bishop-Bond* touches the nerve of what it means to grow up black, harboring stereotypical views of family origin and status through time and locale. Through his persistent research and meticulous documentation, Reggie Bishop has turned many long-held stereotypical assumptions on their heads. The reader is taken through the author's personal lifelong challenges and struggles as he exemplifies generation by generation how his forbearers met and overcame the odds. One cannot miss the uniqueness of pursuit of African American family history, nor but marvel at the personal commitment and sense of obligation to record the stories."

J. Arch Phillips
Past President, Harford County Genealogical Society

THE
BISHOP
BOND

REGGIE BISHOP

THE
BISHP
BOND

Finding Yourself through Your Family Roots

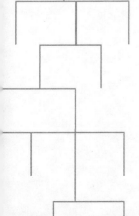

TATE PUBLISHING
AND **ENTERPRISES**, LLC

Published by Tate Publishing & Enterprises, LLC

127 E. Trade Center Terrace | Mustang, Oklahoma 73064 USA
1.888.361.9473 | www.tatepublishing.com

Tate Publishing is committed to excellence in the publishing industry. The company reflects the philosophy established by the founders, based on Psalm 68:11,

"The Lord gave the word and great was the company of those who published it."

Book design copyright © 2012 by Tate Publishing, LLC. All rights reserved.
Cover design by Joel Uber
Interior design by Rtor Maghuyop

Published in the United States of America
ISBN: 978-1-62024-446-3

Library of Congress Control Number: 2012944886

1. Reference / Genealogy & Heraldry
2. Biography & Autobiography / Personal Memoirs
12.07.09

DEDICATION

I dedicate this book to my niece, nephews, sister, aunts, and uncles, kinship links to the Bishop-Bond union. I dedicate this book to my mom for being remarkably faithful. Also, many thanks to "Mom" Millie and the New Writers in Action group for reading parts of the story to me.

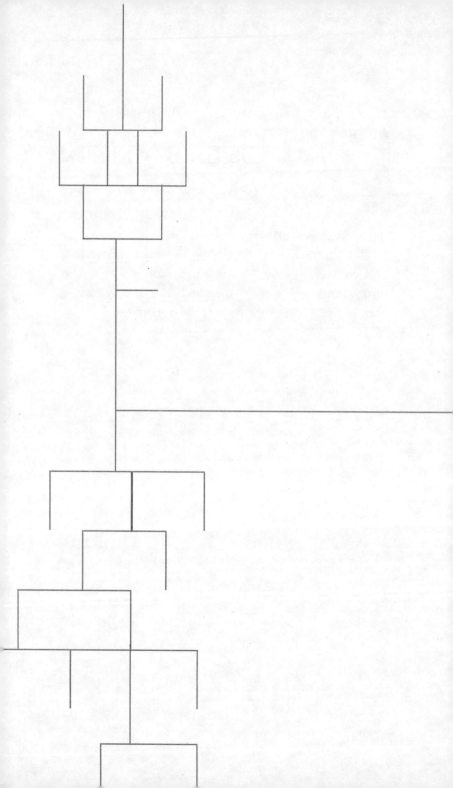

TABLE OF CONTENTS

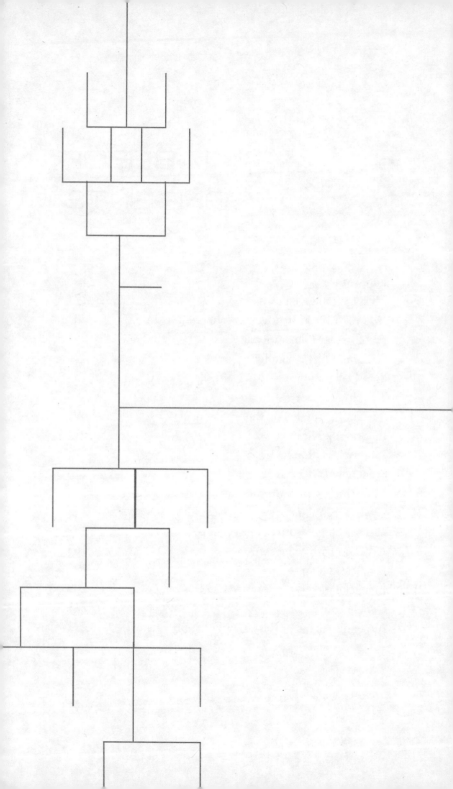

FOREWORD

When I met this author, Mr. Bishop, I felt an obligation to reach out to him, because he was embarking upon a journey that was inspiring, and since I had traveled this road before, I knew it wasn't going to be easy. So, instantly, he became special to me, like a son. I wanted to mentor him, because I could see his passion in his work in finding his family connections. The joy in his face was like a light that would beam in the dark of night. I remember thinking, *His family must be so proud of him, because he is the array of hope, love, and understanding for them.*

I am proud of his persistence in bringing this work to a finished product and to see the hope in his eyes that this would become a beacon to his family's connections that would move them forward into the future, loving one another.

It's a pleasure to write this foreword for a work that's worthy of praise. Books about family connection have always brought joy to my heart, because I believe we are nothing without family. The Bishop and Bond families will see the love that the author put into this work and how much he loves his family. *The Bishop Bond: Finding Yourself through Your Family Roots* will touch the hearts of many and give them encouragement to embark upon finding their family connections.

Mentoring, reviewing, and watching Reggie work on *The Bishop Bond: Finding Yourself through Your Family Roots* takes on life of its own, which brought me hope to continue my passion.

—Ms. Millie L. McGhee
Author

MESSAGE TO MY FAMILY

"We Are Who We Are, As Links of One Another."

The Bishop-Bond family tree is huge, and its roots grow deep but are firmly grounded; as branches fade and break away, the foundation remains and cannot be uprooted. The family tree continues to grow as the generation levels increase in tier and branches as the years go by. These branches, the younger generations, will never experience the love, life, and strength of our family role models like those of us who are older. In your hand is my legacy for you to cherish, be inspired, and take in its lessons. Please continue to document your treasure trove of family legacies. This book is a start, and I hope it inspires and you learn from it as I have. The family book is in your hands, written words by yours truly. For many of you, it's not what you expected. The task is somewhat overwhelming for me as I press on to its conclusion. I am blessed every day in what I have learned and what I will learn researching our family history, linking generation to generation.

Abundant blessings to all with love,
Reggie

Surely, "it is what it is," my story to tell, and it's true. I was born this way, with an old mind in a young child's body. Ever since I could remember, family has been important to me. So I spent many years with family and friends, collecting bits of information and skimming through old, dusty documents. Yes, I'm a young man with a mind way beyond my years. I know most of you are reading this because you need encouragement to tell your story, some are just curious, and many of you want to find your roots and become the family's storyteller. I love being the family's storyteller, but I like to call myself the family's historian.

First, before I tell you all the wonderful and some sad things about me and my journey in finding my family roots, let me introduce myself to you. My name is Reginald Bishop, and I was born in Havre de Grace, Maryland, on October 16, 1964. My family often called me "Ol' Man" or "Pops," nicknames assigned to me out of a sense of respect. As a child, elders would point out a sense of wisdom and strength far beyond my years. For some reason, from early childhood, these names never bothered me. I grew to appreciate them, especially now as I research my family history.

At this point in my life, I know there are many things I can share with you, and within these pages, I do. Most importantly, I am a survivor. First, I live by the grace of God, and I love the purpose of being chosen by Him as He intends for us all.

The story you are about to read is my legacy. It is the result of research through my eyes from many years of researching my family's roots. I began to develop this curiosity as a young child, and now as an adult, I am even more fascinated.

I found looking for my ancestors as a great source of finding myself, and now I want to share my thoughts, as well as my views, of what family has meant to me.

A few years ago, I took on the task of seriously seeking out the history of the Bishop/Bond family. My father was a Bishop, and his mother's family was the Bonds. Even though I technically lived in the town of Havre de Grace, I grew up in a modest village a few miles away. This village is where the Bishop and Bond family lived. As a child playing throughout the village, I felt secure knocking on relatives' doors throughout the area. A church was at the center, surrounded by wooded gravel pits and one dirt road. For many years I have been intrigued by the generations of family who had lived in this village.

I wanted to know more about how our family line, the Bishop and the Bond sides, connected with the past of this small community. My plan was to use the words I learned from relatives and the stories of many events witnessed. One part of the Bishop family owned half of the riverside town. Another story talked about to this day is the Bond family having huge cookouts for busloads of Negro soldiers during WWII. Those were things that were the force behind my wanting to find documents that would confirm our family history.

As I listened to stories, I could see that obvious questions needed to be answered or confirmed, and my curiosity piqued to the point of restlessness. I always felt that we have a strong family, and I wanted to do research to find out who we really are. I am amazed today at the many roles in life my relatives have taken on. We are mentors and role models to others. We are Christian ministers and builders of character.

We are musicians and mechanics with a sense of how to make things work. We are founders and pioneers with courage to go where none have gone before. We are teachers and soldiers on the battlefield for education and life's lessons. We are trustees and stewards, stable with concern for maintenance and upkeep. We are free people of color, leaders in difficult times, and originally slaves who endured despite attempts to disenfranchise and strip away who we are.

I wanted to know how we were specifically connected. My family was an anchor throughout times of community blood, sweat, and tears. I am grateful that we were united through difficult times. We are connected to a community and an overall sense of family. We are connected through common organizations, like the school and the church. We are connected by collective situations of segregation and social plight. God has connected to our family through natural kinship.

My family research has allowed me to realize that we come from strong, resilient people. We come from a small town and city along a major river. We come from a big city with advanced and busy ways. On the other hand, we come from a village that was a safe haven of liberation once owned by freed slaves and known as a "freedmen's community." For many generations, as an independent class within American society, we were born free people of color.

Today we have a difficult time holding on to what our forefathers struggled and sacrificed for to provide for future generations. When I look at our family as a whole, I see we purchased our freedom from slavery and we purchased land before the Civil War. We even built churches and schools that exist today in one form or another. Because of this, I am convinced that there's written proof of our families' past that serves as a practical foundation to strengthen the generations for the future.

Many questions may never be answered. Many connections may not be made because of inconsistencies or little to no documentation. My natural curiosity and great passion, nonetheless, for family history have driven me to extensive research. I have collected this information to share my passion and spark others' interest in compiling family histories. My passion, which began as an overnight hobby, has consumed my life. I make no claims of being an expert, but I do know that this is the single most fulfilling accomplishment I have made in life. I learned, through history, the countless rewards of patience and persistence. As I took notes step-by-step in the research process, I discovered there are many things, terms, and techniques I did not know, such as the various forms of identifications, like certificates of freedom or Soundex numbers used on our driver's licenses today. I learned lessons in historical facts of when certain documents used were initiated and later became accessible. For example, present birth certificates are not available to the public for one hundred years and were first issued in the late 1890s.

I hope that my dedication to this book and my committing the words to paper will inspire members of other families to pick up the same excitement that I have had while researching and exploring our family history in Harford County, Maryland. Furthermore, my wish is to guide those just beginning and those who have become stalled in tracing their family roots.

I collected the information based on names, times, and places within a geographic area. By researching local histories, evidence is revealed through the lives of everyday people, which eventually led to information on specific ones, like my family. Obviously, this research is not conclusive. My research is ongoing, and historical information is endlessly being revealed. This is our heritage to be used as a base to build on for those family members interested in continuing to make connections and document and gather family history.

As I get older, I become even more amazed at the community in which I had grown up. The network of who knew who and the warm feeling of closeness at gatherings seem somewhat mystical to me now. The community bond at social events, civil meetings, and religious services always seemed to have a sense of togetherness, like a family reunion. Obviously, this sense had occurred from decades or even centuries of shared community concerns and surviving in hostile situations. Slavery divided the races, estranged families, and stained the history of humanity. Through it all, despite the oppressions imposed on one race of people, these difficulties bind a commonality as a people, linking a closeness of concern and empowerment for the well-being of family and the community at large. Today that warm sense has faded as circumstances have changed, as the world has grown larger, as people move about the country, and as values change. The message of this book is that sense of community can be renewed; it can be revitalized and promoted. It may never absolutely be restored; however, the process of reclamation begins with a firm grasp of one's roots, like the extensive bonds of the Bishop and Bond families.

"MAN IS LIKE
A BREATH..."
(PSALM 144:4, NKJV)

I recall a statement made by my paternal grandfather: "You kids are related to all of Harford County." Today, my conclusion is that his statement is truer than not. Early land records show free persons of color owning a considerable amount of land. It turns out that our family is among these persons, long before the Civil War and connected to the Revolutionary War. The existence of these communities from which we have come has strong, deep, extensive roots and family ties. Our family, reaching out to others with helping hands, has unified the sense of family within the community. This is what we have: a unique bond within our communities, touching and inspiring lives.

As time goes on by, I often wonder what it would have been like to live during my grandparents' childhoods. Who would I have met in my grandfather's family? The Bishops, who were believed to be free, indentured servants. My grandmother's family, the Bonds, was believed to have been devoted leaders in religion and education throughout the community. Would I have lived in a big house; in a shack in Philadelphia, Pennsylvania; or on an island in the West Indies?

When I was a child attending church, elders and members often mentioned one-room schoolhouses. They would mention the potbelly stove, particular gatherings, and the ringing of the church bell on Sunday mornings and special occasions. Obviously, these mementos no longer exist and are hardly mentioned today. However, unlike items that can be historically preserved, it is easy to see how people become nameless and forgotten over time.

My intent is to trace back and reveal as much as possible about the real treasures in my family history: the people and events of our family members, preserving a memorial of encouragement for present and future generations. Like this family, others will see that, if not by blood; we are connected and joined by a source bonded through people, places, and events that occurred generation to generation.

Many family and friends have told me how reluctant their parents were to share any information on family, such as grandparents or great-grandparents and so on. My experience has taught me there are many additional ways to obtain a treasure trove of historical information for those who care to explore, such as searching family stories to draw out clues, revealing a remarkable trail to your heritage, and discovering unique papers to trace your family roots. You too should realize your family history can be unveiled.

I have come to realize how the passage of time has made a change in so many ways. It is hard for me to believe I have reached the prime of my life and am near a half-century old. I recall a conversation as a child with my ninety-year-old great-uncle one autumn morning. We slowly walked in the church grove on a deep layer of fallen acorns from very old oak trees. I would get as close as possible to him to hear his whisper of a voice, and with each step we made, there were loud crunches from our footsteps crunching the acorns. There was a layer heavier than usual covering the entire ground. I tuned in in order to listen intently to him as he said, "We are in for a long, hard winter, but we will get by. My, how time goes on by the older you get."

I have lived to realize "time waits for no one" is purely true. This single memory is as vivid now as it was over forty years ago. My memories and community stories of family are the threads that fuel the search into my family history. Now I wish I could have retained every precious, special moment. I cherish my family memories, and I record every piece I can of the treasure trove of history to preserve the connection from generation to generation.

It is evident to me that change comes in many ways: in the different people we know, the various places we live, and in each growing generation. As we go about our daily lives, I can see a difference time makes. The generation born today in the twenty-first century, the new millennia, is unlike those born in previous generations and my generation. I am convinced time has made a change in the way we do, see, and feel about things. The Internet age has integrated and come to dominate our lives via iPhones, iPads, and other web-based devices, which have become a resource of digital information. As I think of the various devices and technologies used today, I cannot help but think about the trails of data being left behind for future generations of genealogists. Searching for one name in Google results in an infinite amount of information. A click of the computer keys, touch of a screen, or the recognition of a voice command help a person retrieve information for many types of research.

With the remarkable advances in technology, I surmise present generations are unknowingly leaving trails of historical information via social network profiles, blogs, tweets, and various other online media outlets. The Internet with digital technology is rapidly becoming an integral part of our daily lives. This new era now, in its infancy, will link past, present, and future as time leaves its trail in history. A journal, diary, scrapbook program, and personal biography are the start of collecting family mementos to research one's family history. When I started my research into my family history, technology and data were not so advanced. Tedious as it may have been, the thrill of searching through actual scrapbooks, dusty boxes, and packed-away photo albums triggered obscured memories of my family history.

While I was growing up, my rural town in Maryland was a close-knit community (village), and it was customary for a young African American person to address a close elder within the village as "aunt" or "uncle," whether or not they were truly related. Out of traditional respect, we addressed one another in titles, as generic as some may be, like "Pop So-and-So" or "Mom." That is who they were in our close-knit community.

When I was in a store or even at school, it would not be strange to hear someone yell out, "Hey, cuz." "Hey, cuz" often replayed in my mind, like a bee buzzing around my head long after it was gone. I heard the words so often. With my analytical mind, I needed to know how we were cousins, connected, or even related. I would ask my father if we were related to this person and that person.

He would always say, "Yes, on Pop's, your grandfather's, side somehow," with no other details or comments. As time went on, I decided to do serious research into tracing my roots. Research is the hunt for knowledge, an analyzed search designed with an open mind to secure facts, to assess assumptions. The major points of research are evaluation, documentation, discovery, and interpretation expanding what is vaguely known. Specifically, tracing your family roots is an extraordinary journey. The driven pursuit to detect noted trails in time reveals historical treasures to what and who you are. Thus, I set out tracing my African American family roots.

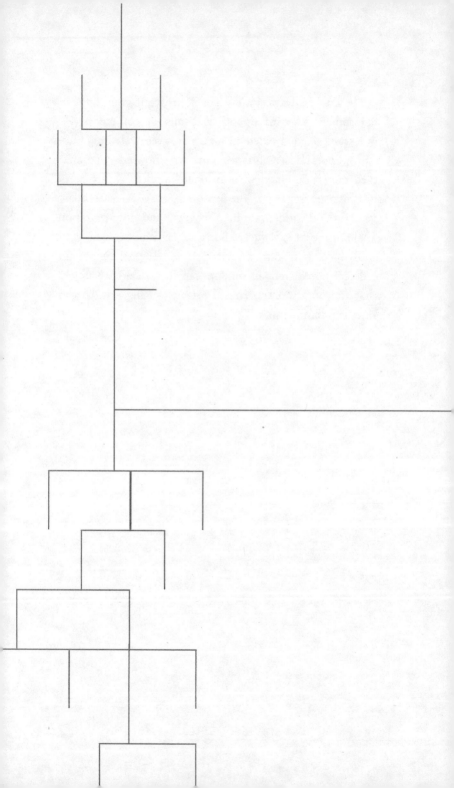

PRESENT-DAY GENERATIONS

I think of the generation of my niece and nephew as the present generation. I think about how, as we journey through life, we leave footprints in time. Sometimes these marked trails are left intentionally, like in a personal journal, scrapbook, or biography; other times they are left unintentionally during our day-to-day activities. As a family historian, I have learned to observe life like a travel plan that leads successfully to and from the destination. Tracing ancestors back from present-day generations is an amazing investigative journey.

Recently, I attended an elementary school program. The printed handout listed the date, location, and complete names of the participants by individual class grade. I recognized a name within the third-grade class as that of my nephew, Brandon. My sister's son is very inquisitive. When he speaks, you think you're talking to a teenager instead of a nine-year-old. He is observant and not shy about asking a question, no matter how silly it may be. In many ways, he reminds me of my dad, his grandfather.

My nephew's generation was the first to be born in the twenty-first century. Cell phones, computers, and the Internet are the norm for them. I saw him with earphones and a microphone playing a game on the television. I did not realize he and a remote friend were playing the same game and they conversed through the earphone. What a different world from when his grandfather's mother was born one hundred years ago at the beginning of the last century. She had neither phone nor electricity, and the norm was limited to walking visits to her close-knit family and friends close by. Recognition of a different time interwoven and layered provides a foundation to get to our present place and generation.

My nephew's printed school program documented for future generations that on this day at this school, nine-year-old Brandon first performed exceptionally as master of ceremony in a segment of his school's special event. I pulled out detailed proof of historic value that marked a special personal trail in time for his family and future generations to come.

Recently, my niece wanted to come home from college in Delaware, and she needed me to come get her. Even though I had not ever been to the campus, I agreed. I was confident, relying on the new GPS navigation device, which I was anxious to use. After an hour of driving, however, the GPS system failed. I was lost, and my niece was packed and readily waiting for me in front of her dorm. I had neither a written address nor a map to get to the college. I stopped at a gas station; unfortunately, they had no maps, and no one had any idea of where the college was. To my surprise, the next gas station had a very expensive map. I cautiously scanned it just to find the directions to the college and was on my way.

My low-budget, outdated cell phone has no bells or advanced whistles, but it definitely rang each time my impatient niece called. She wondered where I was and why I was taking so long. Finally, after about three hours of driving, I arrived, hoping she knew how to get home. Of course she did not, and I had to rely on memory and landmarks, like railroad tracks, corner food stores, and highway signs, to eventually lead us home.

Similar to this trip to an unknown place, family history often involves situations where advanced technology will not do. One illustration involves looking through worn-out, dusty documents from un-scanned files in the basement of the courthouse. Here, one can discover family links through the trail of records that confirm many time-honored stories. I sought out information through letters to archives and historical societies, patiently waiting months for replies to my inquiries. The process is similar to a fact-finding reporter investigating a high-profile case. I expect to be accurate in collecting and uncovering all information for the family history. I can see now, with the advancement in technology today, there will be even more data footprints left for future genealogists to collect.

The lifestyle of the present-day generation is unlike any other in history. In an instant, information and material can be readily available. The process of finding the resource and creating and applying time to put things together has advanced to ready-made items ordered at a click of a button. I am impressed with the advancement of computers and the connection to information by the Internet. At times I am overwhelmed at the technological lessons in order to get actual usage. As I used to look around for a nice produce stand for fresh fruit and vegetables to create my meal, this generation has ready-made food delivered directly to their doors. Where are the kids playing together in areas within their neighborhoods? I rarely see any gathering to play a game of football and baseball. Kids, and any connections they forge, often do so indoors.

This generation lets me know how old I am. My parents took in cousins to care for, with me to help keep them busy; today this generation seems to have no time and concern for being role models for their younger generations. Growing up, my cousins often came over to our house, and I would visit them also. I fear that this generation hardly knows their cousins and younger relatives.

I am very close to my cousins; as a matter of fact, most of them are like brothers and sisters. Their children and children's children often call me "Uncle." Some of them have even had me help them with their history school project on family. I was extremely excited to share detailed history on our family, hoping not to overwhelm the youngster. I enjoy seeing the young people's expressions when classmates of my niece and nephew turn out to be five and six generations from the Bishop-Bond union almost a century ago.

Growing up along the tranquil Susquehanna River was a very laid-back and peaceful experience. During my youth, there was not much traffic. As I walked along the banks of the river, a remnant of much busier and more active times was overgrown within the brush. Hidden within the heavily wooded overgrowth is a trail of rusted railroad tracks and antiquated metal objects. As I walked beneath the modern steel bridge that crossed the river, I could not help to daydream of times past in steam engine locomotives and motion of people who once traveled this same, now abandoned railroad track many decades before.

Interwoven in our present existence is evidence of a time long past, now the debris of forgotten, corroded metal of junk disconnected from ever having been useful to people of earlier life. I was always an inquisitive child, often intrigued by those remnants of the past the piqued a sense of curiosity in my mind for the people and things that had handled them in preceding generations. I saw these vestiges as links to me and my generation to generations of the past and to those in the future.

Sociologists refer to my generation as the "Post-Boomers" or "Gen X," claiming we do not know who we are, where we are going, just flowing with the wind of society's ways. I think I was left out of my own generation or was just unique and not persuaded to be like my generation of peers. Family repeatedly said I was beyond my years in the way I did and said things.

As a child, I was not much of a conversationalist, just a thinker pondering things analytically in my mind. It was instinctive to me to research ideas and thoughts that came to mind in the library or encyclopedia. As I grew implementing ideas into a well-planned, beautiful garden and raising broods of tropical African fish, I experienced success and failures along the way. Even with much thought and design, I realized things often do not always go the way I had meticulously planned.

Inherited characteristics are integrated in our lives and are not by our own design. The Divine sets them like tracks to reach a particular, purposed destination; it is not always seen by ourselves but noticed by others. I have a difficult time describing myself. When people ask for a biography or formal introduction, I rely on others who have lived around me to write something. In many cases, I do not have to ask, like in this tribute given to me from a dear and wonderful, unrelated mother of my church.

"Noble"
Reginald, you are a noble,
outstanding young man.
I believe you are living your life
according to God's commands

You are always looking
for ways to serve God,
not for an outside show
but from the bottom of your heart

You are kind and giving, faithful and true
You truly make an effort to let the Lord use you
and God won't forget your acts of kindness and
love
as he smiles down on you from heaven above

I'm sure it makes your mother proud
as the days go by
to have such a wonderful son
on whom she can rely

Reggie, we love you,
and God loves you too in all your trials and
tribulations,
He will bring you through

You have a nice personality
so keep that smile on your face
May God give you your heart's desire
as he pours out his mercy and grace."

—Beulah Burns

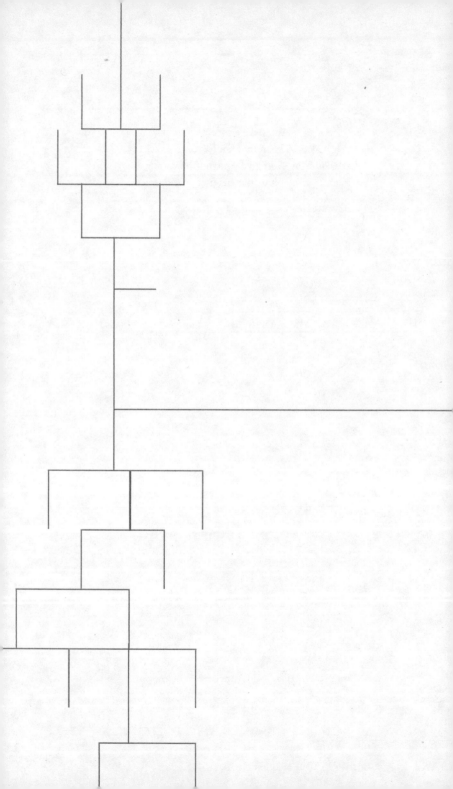

A COMMUNITY,
A FAMILY

Our neighborhood within Havre de Grace was a close-knit community. If someone died or needed help, a couple of ladies would walk door-to-door to let one another know in order for families to help out with food, money, or comfort. We kids could do no wrong without someone making sure our parents knew what we had done. For the most part, we did not get into too much trouble. If we were not at the marble tree, we would be in front of my house playing games, like four squares or riding bikes, skateboarding, or, at times, pitching coins at the curb of the newly paved road in front of our house.

The home I grew up in was a modest three-bedroom home on Garfield Road next to the bridge on Route 40, crossing over the Susquehanna River. I remember the road being a dirt road that was often sprayed down with oil to keep dust from going everywhere. The dangerous traffic coming off the bridge from Perryville ramped directly into our neighborhood on Park Drive. I recall many terrible accidents there. Finally, after several years, road crews put in sidewalks and paved our road. It seemed like a huge celebration. It was not uncommon for a dozen kids to be in front of our house at any given time. Even so, when our road had been newly paved, several dozen kids came from all over to skateboard down the road's incline. Kids I normally would see only in school would be there. Furthermore, cousins joined in from Churchville, Aberdeen, and as far as Chester, Pennsylvania, for the thrill of going fast down an incline on skateboards.

I was never a daredevil, and I was always overly cautious in all that I did. Our road ended at the bottom of the incline that intersected with Park Drive. The result of starting at the top of the incline on a skateboard was not being able to stop at the intersection for traffic or even the curb. Many kids crashed into the curb, tumbling over the paved road onto the grassy field. I often watched from the steps of our house. I only rode my skateboard down the incline a few times, and even then I was sitting on it and could stop using both feet already close to the road. I did not care too much for the skateboard anyway; it was too much work. I'd rather ride my bike.

As most of the neighborhood boys, including my brother, played football in the grassy field, I was content with playing board games. I had several board games, like checkers, Pay Day, Trouble, and many others. Friends and I would sit for hours in front of the house playing them. Then playing marbles became my game. In the grassy field were several pine trees, and we had chosen the largest as our neighborhood-centered meeting place. I had great times just meeting to hang out, sharing stories of school and new toys. We often compared newfound hobbies and talked about sports. I just wanted to play marbles to add to my huge collection.

I suppose collecting as many marbles as I could from other people and trading them off gave us individually a sense of superiority. I seemed to thrive off of it. The power of winning other people's marbles, especially the special ones with beautiful colors and unique designs, was gratifying. Winning someone's special marble in a good game with a half dozen boys was clear, public proof of my outright win. Showing off the special marble was very rewarding. Collecting marbles gave me an edge and a well-deserved right to brag expressed not only verbally but by showing off my huge collection of beautiful designed marbles. The game could get quite intense at times. It's not comfortable giving up what was rightfully yours. We all had to yield reluctantly to the rules of the game from time to time. Many times behind the scene, I would trade a person's special marble back to them for several others. My nephew now has part of my collection of marbles kept over the many years in a tin cocoa can. Memories remain, but sadly the neighborhood is not what it used to be, and the marble tree is gone.

Many of the same boys meeting under the marble tree and playing and tumbling off skateboards into the grassy field went on to join the Little League football team, which my father coached consistently for many years. On the other hand, I joined the early junior bowling league, which met every Saturday morning. The rest of my family was involved with the newly active football league in one form or another. My mom worked at times at the concession stand and helped out where it was needed. My brother played along with my cousin, being about the same age on a team together. Over a number of years, as the successful youth program grew, my sister became part of its cheerleaders. One year various teams came from other states, and two boys in my brother's age group stayed with us overnight. I believe the two boys felt welcome and warm in our home, as they were family for that short time.

As a child, I was shy and very curious in my own quiet way. I never looked for attention, always content with what came my way. Even though I was the oldest of three children, my silence was ruling—ruling in the sense that when I said something, I certainly meant what I said, and there was a definite purpose for me speaking, like someone asking me a direct question. Hardly ever imposing, I often waited for an invitation to join in. I seemed to get along with everyone, no matter who they were. I could care for the young and serve the old. It did not matter what they did. My interest or hobbies varied. I could pass the time away with whatever was before me. I guess that had been from my early school years of being introduced to the various creative activities that I certainly enjoyed.

I enjoyed my first year in elementary school. I remember the sandbox, Play-Doh, paints, and the board game Candy Land. While I was having a good time attending school that first year, I did not realize just four years earlier that schools were segregated in Harford County. In 1965, all-black schools and all-white schools merged into one school system, ending segregation

I have fond memories of my early school years that I can vividly picture in my mind. Most of those years were pleasant with little regret of childhood blunders. Not mischievous in any way, I was much too nervous and overly honest to do or say anything fallacious. The only thing I can recall being guilty of is taking a long while to use the bathroom.

In first grade, the first year to attend school all day, I remember many friends fondly. The school had a parental visitation day, and to my surprise, my father came to see me. I was so happy to see him, although being in the room with all my new friends and classmates was demanding. I had to keep my composure and be a good schoolboy. Well, I am not sure what came over me, but for some reason or another, I lost control. To this day, I blame it on my nerves. From out of nowhere, I began to uncontrollably cry, and if that wasn't bad enough, I became sick. My breakfast, lunch, snacks, and all I had eaten was all over the back of the room and hall of the school. I was fine when we got home. As for my dad, I suppose he was too embarrassed to visit me in school ever again. He categorically avoided unpleasant things of all sorts and all types.

Nobility is a value I inherited from preceding ancestors who laid a firm, loyal foundation for each succeeding generation. I am the oldest child of three children, born to George and Anne Lewis-Bishop in Havre de Grace, Maryland. My brother, Derwin Maurice Bishop, died in May 1994 at age twenty-eight years of age with no children. Without getting help, he had lost too much blood from severely lacerating himself on a broken glass windowpane. I was very sad for the loss of my brother. However, my father was far more deeply afflicted and grief-stricken.

We called my brother "Reesie," and he and I were totally opposite in many ways. He was very athletic, slightly shorter than me by inches, with smooth, dark skin and naturally curly hair. Like our father, he lived to work on and build high-performance cars. On the other hand, I did not have any interest in any mechanical vehicles other than them getting me to where I needed to go. I recall sharing a room with Reesie growing up and listening to automobiles passing by, and he could name the year, make, and model of each one we heard. Totally bored, not knowing any vehicles, I would charitably act if I was interested. I often agreed with his chattering to encourage him until we both fell asleep.

As a child my little sister, Nerissa, seemed to me to be quite the character. Some of the dramatic things she would do as a little girl would make me think she was an award-winning actress. Serious but not overbearing, she could have fun make-believing all by herself. Her privacy was very important to her. She kept her room door closed, like she was hiding something special all the time.

One day curiosity got the best of me, and I went on a surveillance mission. I hid and waited in her small cluttered room closet a long time to see what her closely guarded secret was. To my surprise, peeping through cracks in the closet curtain, I saw her in action and could not contain myself. I tried to hold my laughter so hard that I was in extreme pain. I fell out through the closet to the floor, crying in laughter. Behind her closed doors, Rissa's imagination abounded; she was being the best dramatic and flamboyant actress, performing with unseen friends the world would never see. She had the voices for all her imaginary playmates.

My siblings and I have many distinct traits, personalities, and characteristics. If we had not grown up together, people would not have known us as a family. We were only a few years apart within the same parents and born within the same generation era, yet outwardly we seemed unrelated.

We were nurtured with two parents working regularly and looking out for one another. We had the stability of being raised in one home, surrounded by a close-knit community of family and friends. A path rooted in the past several generations laid our secure foundation. The Bishop-Bond extended foundation, rooted several generations before, was the path to who we have become as a community of family. Even with many characteristic differences, this foundation connects and uniquely links common kinship within the Bishop-Bond family.

My family has faced many challenges and has handled them with a sense of control. Tests like these often bring out the true characters of faith, courage, and rebounding strength. I suppose this trait is most prevalent within me, as I have had to face numerous unfortunate events throughout my life. Things from the outside are not always what they seem. I am known for a big smile all the time; however, internal attacks and misfortunes often bear a toll on me within. I certainly believe my genuine smile is an inherited defense mechanism to cause things to be all right.

A few days before my ninth birthday in October of 1973, I was sitting in the living room watching TV. I recall my father in the kitchen fixing hot dogs or a sandwich to eat. The last thing I can remember was him giving me a donut and root beer soda. After passing out, I awoke asking myself, *What's going on? Why am I extremely thirsty, and who is carrying me around?* These are the thoughts that came to mind as I awoke semiconsciously in the hospital emergency room. I was clutched in the arms of my father. I recall he had a frightening look on his face as I said in a small, raspy voice, "I thirsty."

I remember him carrying me to the water fountain and placing the stream of water on my lips; just then I passed out for a second time. I had awakened in a hard bed with metal bars on the side. I felt as if I had a nice, refreshing nap. Standing over me was a doctor in white with my dad and my mom, who had a gift-wrapped box in her hand. My mouth was extremely dry as I gathered my senses and heard Dad say, "Hey there."

At that moment, the doctor put a large swabbed cotton stick on my lips and tongue. It was good and refreshing on my dry lips. I believe my mom had a white cup of cold water with a straw in it. I took a sip of it, and it was nice and cold. I think I asked for a soda, and someone said I could no longer have any. The doctor said, "You lucky, little turtle dove."

All I knew during that time of serious health crisis was that I got lots of attention for what I thought was little reason. Mom had cards and gifts for me. I wondered if this was what hospital life was all about. I was in no pain despite a tube in my wrist. I was diagnosed with type-one diabetes, where the body completely stops producing the natural hormone, insulin. This chronic medical disorder was particularly serious in that I would need insulin shots daily for the rest of my life.

My aunt said, "You have sugar, like your Mom-Mom Bishop had." Although I did not quite understand, the instructions of food measurements were ever present on menus. A little reality set in when the bland, nasty-tasting food came for me to eat. I most wanted a soda, and a nurse said she would try to get me something called "Tab." In the meantime, she gave me that cotton-tipped stick to soothe and refresh my very dry mouth.

While in the hospital, I had missed my birthday celebration with my school classmates. I remember my mom bringing a bag full of birthday cards and get-well wishes. Despite the food, my stay in the hospital was enjoyable. It had a playroom, and I learned to draw cartoon characters, like Snoopy from *Charlie Brown*. The nurses were nice and soon gave me a cup of diet cola soda called "Tab," which tasted okay.

I have warm memories of elementary school, despite diabetes. I had such wonderful teachers who were very kind and taught lessons creatively. I do not think I was ever bored. Even summer school was fun, even though we had to find our way there by whatever means necessary. Sometimes I would catch a ride with family or ride my bike. On good days, we often walked the steep, graded hill with neighborhood friends. We dared not walk alone, for there was security in numbers to watch each other, I was told. All the neighborhood kids together protected one another and warned each other of weird strangers who wished to do us harm. Even with our numbers of seven or more, fear was inevitably at the top of the hill to school. Like a starting gun at the beginning of a race, we always knew at the iron fence's edge, someone instantly would say, "Run, run as fast as you can!"

At the corner several yards from the school, we would rejoice with victorious hugs as the last person touched the others. There was no praise or honor for whoever came in first; we were all relieved to have finished. With great laughter, we often entered summer school knowing we had escaped the scary clutches of the old, white, ghost-looking trees in the ancient cemetery. I actually did not have any problems with the cemetery. There were days the other kids left me behind because I did not feel like running. Furthermore, in the wintertime, when snow covered the cemetery, we all had a great time sleighing, hitting tombstones, trees, and all with no fear. We were all together, looking out for one another as close friends and family.

Our small community knew one another and stretched into learning with others. I enjoyed school when the teacher would read books out loud in class as we lay our heads on the desk, visualizing the stories like *Charlotte's Web* and *Moby Dick*. My love for gardening started in the classroom when we would plant seeds in a paper cup and then plant them in the school garden or take them home to plant. The school had a beautiful courtyard, with spring blooming flowers in it. Throughout the small school, a sense of family was highly cultivated with parent interaction and participation.

Oh, I almost forgot. My dad did have to come back to my elementary school for a rescue from that courtyard. It happened one sunny day when I was walking in the hall to the cafeteria for my morning snack. Yes, being the only kid with diabetes granted me special privileges. Our school had a closed-in courtyard, and walking the halls, on each side you bypass it. Lo and behold, there was something big moving in it this day. I immediately ran to the office to tell them that "Bill is in the courtyard!"

The principal, who often joined me during my snack breaks, came out of his office and said, "Does he belong to you?"

To my great surprise, my big, old, mixed-breed mutt of a dog had followed the bus to school that day. They said he leisurely walked in like he was a good student looking to learn. The principal had locked him in the courtyard until finding out what to do with him. He was in there all day long, with the whole school knowing his name and who he belonged to, especially the kids who knew him from the neighborhood who had seen him. All day the kids chatted and would say, "Your dog came to school" or "Your dog is in the courtyard."

I would reply, "I know it. That's my wonder dog, Bill."

The office called my father. Bill had to wait until late that evening when my father got off from work to be rescued from the courtyard and brought home in the pickup truck.

A few years earlier, Bill was a huge, mean-looking dog. I was four years old when my father and mother purchased the home I grew up in. As we looked outside through the dining room window, we could see a dog chained to his doghouse. A very old couple lived there named Mr. and Mrs. Calendar. I remember Bill always being tied up next to his doghouse in the backyard. I never saw anyone—not even the couple—interact with him. He was a huge, ugly dog, a possible mix of German shepherd, Saint Bernard, beagle, and whatever else. I know I was scared of him. I remember playing with some neighborhood friends near the fence and Bill acted like he wanted to play along with us.

I was about seven or eight years old when the couple was no longer living at the home. I assumed they had died or were placed in a nursing home together. The dog was abandoned and tied up, and he had no one to feed or take care of him. One day he broke loose and was sitting on our front porch. My brother and I debated about who was going out there first. We yelled and screamed all kinds of crazy things, and Bill would not move nor make a sound. We knew Dad would be home soon, so we waited, terrified to go outside and held hostage inside by a huge, ugly, crazy-eyed dog sitting on our porch. Mom was preoccupied sewing together a dress or outfit of some kind. She had nothing to do with animals of any kind, wild or domestic.

My brother and I kept busy in our room playing games and listening to music. We forgot all about being held hostage until we heard my father's voice; he was home from work. We both ran to greet him. We asked if he saw Bill, who got loose. He acted like nothing was wrong, going about his regular routine of washing up and fixing a jelly sandwich.

I asked, "Dad, you see that ugly dog loose out there sitting on our steps?"

Dad said, "He is out there walking around hungry. You feed him?"

I screamed, "No way! He's mean and gonna bite me."

Dad told us Bill was gentle as could be and would not harm anyone, and he was going to see if someone wanted him. If not, he was getting rid of him before Mom started complaining about the animal being around.

Slowly but surely, I warmed up to Bill by feeding him and talking to him. He was so timid that at a clap of your hands or loud talking, he would run off and hide.

A few weeks passed before my dad took Bill away. He told me he took Bill up to the country. I automatically assumed he went to my aunt's farm in Jarrettsville, about thirty minutes north of us, and I did not think any more of him.

A few months went by. We all were coming home from somewhere, and Dad pulled in front of the house. There was an emaciated, slow-walking dog on our porch. Dad told us to stay in the car, and he got something to try to chase it away. At first it would not move, sitting and looking wild and crazy, and then suddenly it took off.

I yelled, "It's Bill!"

My brother said, "You crazy; it's not him."

Dad came back all out of breath from chasing the dog off somewhere. I told him I thought it was Bill. He said it couldn't be and that he had dropped him off up in Pennsylvania on the other side of the river above the Conowingo Dam, approximately twenty miles away through a rough wooded area.

A few days later, I was sitting out in the yard quietly reading, and I felt a presence. It was the dog watching me. I was scared at first, hearing about wild animals and rabies and such. I whispered, "Bill," and he walked slowly toward me. I said, "It's okay, Bill."

I turned the water on, and he drank. My loudmouthed brother came, and Bill ran again.

That night I told Dad and put some leftover food out. Bill came back, and I slowly started cleaning him up. The next day my dad took him to the vet and was amazed. Despite two buckshot bullets, he was healthy. Mom was puzzled. The whole episode convinced her to say nothing derogatory about the dog. I was elated to see this scared, timid dog return to the only real family he had ever known.

Even though as a family we were reluctant to accept him at first, Bill became part of our family and was my wonder dog for years. I have come to recognize that whether it is an animal, a neighbor, or even a stranger, ingrained within my family is a will to help through caring, nurturing, and being unified in a sense of kinship. Like Bill, uniquely drawn back to that special place, the spirit of family draws stranger, orphan, and stray animals to know where home is. Despite differences, family is unique in that a special bond of security and comfort is rekindled when contacted after being out of touch or a part a while.

After more than a year of having diabetes, I was sent off to attend a summer camp for children with diabetes. It was my first time away from all my family. Indeed, I was looking forward to being at camp with other kids. For some reason, suddenly, at one point, Mom and Dad stood at the camp bunk door. I cried. It was an uncontrollable response that welled up from out of nowhere. After a short moment, it was out of my system for good, and I laughed.

The camp, known as "Camp Glyndon," was located about fifty miles away from home in Baltimore County. I was surrounded by kids of every age with girls and boys of varying backgrounds with one commonality: diabetes. I enjoyed camp for two whole weeks, swimming, wrestling, riding horses, playing various games, and hearing camp ghost stories while also learning to manage diabetes. Before attending camp, I was unable to give myself insulin shots. I never could get the nerve to stab myself with a long, sharp needle, even after practicing a long while on an orange. At camp, after seeing younger kids giving their own shots, I had to prove I could. I thought, *Those little guys are not going to outdo me.*

The first morning, the counselor asked if I could give my own shots. I lied and said I could when I knew I had never stabbed myself before. When I proved myself honest and gave my own shot anyway for the first time, I was astonished. It was not as injurious as my mind led me to believe. Furthermore, I think the counselor knew it was my first time because of the look of glee on my blushing face through the big smile. I attended camp for two years, meeting good friends while learning a lot in managing diabetes. I was even voted the best camper and brought home a trophy each year from among the twenty campers within our bunk house of about ten others in the entire camp. I was not the best diabetes patient but, like my father, I was a people person with a caring spirit and support of family and friends all around me.

Growing up with a hardworking father and mother, I appreciated the stability they provided, especially during episodes of us kids being cantankerous. A strong family support system is crucial in raising young children. A neighborhood of like-minded families added extra support and balance. This overall family structure prevailed within my established African American community well into the time of my high school graduation and college years in the 1980s.

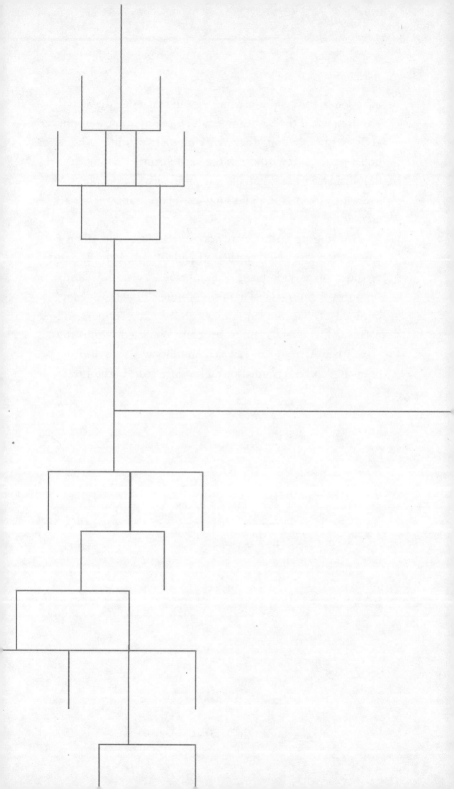

THAT GENERATION

My Dad, the Dreamer

Born during WWII, my father, George Bishop, was the tenth child of thirteen. I always thought my father was exceptionally rare in that he looked to the future with total optimism despite being in a fairly dismal state. My father was an uncomplicated and level-headed family man and a people person. In almost every aspect of his life, he avoided unpleasant things and situations. For instance, I recall him not having anything to do with the strong smells of food, like soul foods and seafood. If someone was loud and belligerent, my father, after trying to calm them down, would walk away.

He could be anywhere and strike up a conversation, leaving everyone uplifted and encouraged to press forward through any difficult situation. My father was a dreamer. I believe he wanted those around him to have what made them the happiest. Often getting them to think, he would provide them with something he could not make happen anytime soon. His life was guided more by ideas than practical considerations, like the promise of a new car or house.

Growing up, I remember him always humming and singing with a smooth, baritone style of a lead singer, like Sam Cooke. He would make up songs from off the top of his head and direct them to the attention of the listener's specific name within the easy-flowing lyrics. Riding in the car, he would instantly break out in a song, and then I would soon hear my name from out of nowhere. My father always looked at us in uplifting affirmation, expressing love for his children and their mother. As children, once we giggled and started getting used to it, the promise of new this or getting that faded from our mental image into hope that may soon be realized.

My father was a dreamer. He often talked about starting a singing group, with my little cousins as band members. Countless times I recall the conversation of a brand-new home with a garage and basement, not to mention having his own tractor-trailer business; this later came at an ultimate, life-changing price.

My father had a passion for sports and was always doing something athletic. On many Monday nights, after working all day, he would hug me and my siblings good night and leave to go to the local bowling lanes and join a league of brothers, cousins, and uncles. I often wanted to go with him to join the guys in the all-black bowling league. He would tell me I could join when I got older.

My father could rally a group of guys together in an instant to play horseshoes or go to the nearest baseball field. I often giggled when he would take me and my brother to the basketball court with cousins. Despite him sometimes being the shortest on the court, every week a group of guys, including his brothers and cousins, would play basketball in a nearby school. If he was not playing a sport, he often coached or watched it on TV with a simple soda, hotdog, donut, or jelly sandwich.

For as long as I can remember, my father was involved in the community. After the integration of schools in the 1960s, he was one of the first and only black coaches for Little League baseball. For several decades, he was coach for the Parks and Recreation programs of baseball, basketball, and football.

On April 9, 1940, my father, George Wesley Bishop, was born to Oscar and Sarah Bishop at 6:40 a.m. in Havre de Grace, Maryland. His birth certificate states his mother lived at her current residence for twelve years and had nine living children. The birth certificate is not available to the public before one hundred years unless it is appointed a personal representative of the estate. My father's birth certificate, acquired from his records to me, substantiates the fact of when his parents moved to the home place in Gravel Hill and the number of siblings born before him.

Born during the time of World War II, my father experienced hard times but also extraordinary gains. The radio increased in popularity with the wiring of electricity throughout the country. Television added visual to the voice of the telephones connecting families and communities in each state. In 1947, Jackie Robinson broke Major League Baseball's color barrier. He, an African American, was the first to be signed to the Brooklyn Dodgers. My father was only seven years old at that time. I actually expect he and his brothers and all other relatives listened on the radio as this major event in black athletic history took place.

I envision my father, the tenth child of thirteen, being surrounded by family, always in the form of siblings, cousins, grandparents, aunts, and uncles. I remember him telling me he was in class with his nephews. His older sisters had children around the time my father was born. I can only imagine the traffic at gatherings within this one household. I can think of the hustle to get ready for school and the competition of sibling rivalry throughout. During his time of school, buses were available to kids in rural areas; even so, the family proudly states the fact of having in-house chauffeurs. Not only did the older brothers have cars, but the grandparents had cars, and my father's mother's brother always had a nice car to take care of what was needed. As a matter of fact, as a teenager, I was visited by my great-uncle, who, at over ninety years old, was still driving.

My father's earliest education started out in a one-room schoolhouse next to the AME church near his home in Gravel Hill. At thirteen, he was in the new Havre de Grace Consolidated School, which served all ages of black students from surrounding villages like Bush Chapel, Gravel Hill, Perryman, Havre de Grace, Hopewell, and Swan Creek. Built in 1953, it combined all the old, run-down, one-room schoolhouses that taught only elementary students at that time. This central learning center, along with community organizations, cultivated a unified sense of family throughout the collective African American people in Eastern Harford County.

As I reminisce of my own childhood, I can imagine my father occupying his time as a youth, especially during long summer days walking throughout the neighborhood and fruit orchards nearby. He said that he and his brothers would often gorge themselves on berries, cherries, pears, and apples on nearby farms before spending summers in New York with his father's sister. She took care of and raised other nephews and stepsons, even though she had no children of her own.

I can remember when I was diagnosed with diabetes receiving the many cards and much sympathy from the community. My neighborhood friends became concerned and offered to help in whatever way they could, not really having an understanding of what was wrong with me at the time. I also did not know how devastating the disease may possibly be. I may have been the youngest diagnosed person with diabetes in the whole community. Not knowing then, I soon learned that my father had experiences with its deadly complications

My father treated me with gentle care and "you-need-anything" kindness. His mother's side of the family dealt with the devastating complications of diabetes, like blindness, amputations, and kidney and heart failures. My father contributed diabetes to the death of his dear mother. On the other hand, my mom was the warrior; she gave me my insulin shots, weighed out my foods, and was a constant source of encouragement as she learned to teach me on a daily basis. She enrolled in college and learned of health and nutrition, which she used to work in our local school cafeteria. She worked, educated, and disciplined her children. My mom complemented my very passive father perfectly, making them a superb, balanced couple.

My father was a dreamer, an athlete, a mentor, and a role model. Often there would be older kids cutting our grass or just spending time around my father as he worked on cars in our driveway. My father had been a coach for Little League baseball and football in Aberdeen, five miles away. He was captain of a men's bowling team and organized weekly basketball games with guys in the community. When the boys in the neighborhood started to get old enough, I am sure he had something to do with Little League football starting in Havre de Grace.

Even though the schools and Little Leagues were integrated, the neighborhood was mostly segregated. Even the military had been integrated prior to my father joining in the late 1950s. I recall my father talking about us being better off than lots of other countries. When he served two years in the army, he was active overseas in other countries. He did not say specifically which ones. I would try to ask about his travels oversea but would only get a vague answer. I only can figure it was too unpleasant for him to even talk about. My mom said he was once stung by a scorpion while lying in an army bunk. All I know is he would write home constantly to his mom during those years of being away, according to family members. I hardly ever saw him write anything, and those letters are long gone now. A short while after returning and being discharged from military service as a mechanic, he met my mom. For years, they both worked within their childhood communities, maintaining a livelihood and defining their place within their own home, beginning a generation and tier of the Bishop-Bond family.

THE
HOME PLACE

Pop-Pop Oscar Bishop and Mom-Mom Sarah Bond-Bishop moved to Maryland in 1928 and resided at Gravel Hill Road in Havre de Grace. According to my father's birth certificate, in April 1940, they lived at rural route RDF#1 for twelve years and made their home among this close-knit village of relatives and friends. In the 1930 census, Oscar J. and Sarah A. are listed with five children and an eighty-one-year-old boarder, Jerry Ellis. Family members say Pop Ellis was a link to cousins within the kinship line of the Ellis family. Research is ongoing to trace the documentation to the story and specific connections of this family branch.

My grandparents, during the 1920s and the Depression, had no stocks and investments or even much money to work with. Pop-Pop Oscar was a general worker during this difficult time. He worked at odd jobs and for private white families. He did what he could to provide for his growing family. During this national crisis, a close-knit community was essential to survival. As the family lived with meager means, little became much when pulled together within a village community. This extended family of neighbors joined together, sharing resources for each other and my grandfather's young family.

My grandparents' Social Security application confirms who they are with a birthdate, parents' names, and where they lived in 1937. Pop Oscar listed his current job as "'W' Plumbing" in Aberdeen and unemployed, which leads me to believe if there was a job, he worked; if not, he did not work. Mom Sarah filed her application in 1938, which listed her present employer as "A. C. Elsner" of Havre de Grace. Mom Sarah worked in fireworks and canning house factories and also worked various jobs as a domestic for private families.

Difficult financial times were no stranger to my grandparents. My grandmother would save and take advantage of all tokens, coupons, or discounts stores allowed. When the nation developed welfare and assistance programs for the disadvantaged, orphaned, and impoverished, my grandfather adamantly refused services. I recall being told an instance of a social services program offering food. As the worker was delivering the food at the door of the home place, Pop-Pop burst into a tirade, cursing and threatening the worker off the porch, chasing him away from the property. Whether out of pride, selfishness, or an overwhelming sense of protection for his family, very few outsiders were welcome at his family's home place.

The home place was an old, hot, and dark two-story house pieced together with updated additions over several years. My little sister was definitely afraid to enter or get near the front porch, which was always buzzing with bees. I often explored the old home with its awkward rooms and unlevel floors. Each room had heavy doors that seemed to be stuck or even blocked with boxes and household goods. My exploration was always shortened by fear of getting caught from the sounding of the ever-creaking floors, revealing my presence throughout the upstairs.

My father's siblings often had impromptu gatherings. It seemed if one knew that another was coming in from out of town, so all the siblings would come together. I believe this closeness and coming together helped this family get through the worst of times.

I always thought I had the kindest and most caring family. If there were any ill-feelings or harshness, I never knew it. Things seemed to be always fine, especially at family gatherings. I remember only peace and tranquility as family sat under the trees on blankets and waited as cars pulled up. Uncles would gleefully run to the car and retrieve a wheelchair. Leisurely anticipating other family to arrive seemed slow in motion until my aunt Celeste, the oldest of the thirteen children, pulled up in her family car.

As the parade of people surrounded her car, my aunt was she reminded me of a fine china doll, so petite and extremely beautiful. She would look at you with a smile, not saying a word, but the look said, "Boy, you better come give me a hug." Traditional greetings of a kiss seemed not enough for most of my family, especially my lovely aunts. I could not help but go and hug her. In the late 1950s, she started falling and read medical books for an explanation. She knew from her research, and the doctor confirmed a diagnosis of MS, multiple sclerosis. In 1941, she had married Arthur Jamison from Jarrettsville, Maryland, and resided in Chester, Pennsylvania. From this union came six children, three boys and three girls, with four tiers of present-day generations.

Aunt Geraldine ("Gerl"), a beautiful model of elegance and collective harmony, resided near the home place for more than eighty years. She, being a steadfast pillar of the community and mother to us all, with her husband, Herman Hague, fully supported many organizations and established activities throughout the community. This couple had three children, two girls and a boy, now with three generations begotten them.

Aunt Alberta ("Bertie"), a studious woman, was a natural-born teacher and very true to her trade. She had a lesson in all she did and said, even to the point of collecting and saving everything. A quiet, kind, and gentle woman, she married Raymond Purnell and lived in Cambridge, Maryland; both were educators. They had two sons, and there are three tiers of generations to this union.

Aunt Jean ("Cina") Acina was a fierce, dauntless, and awesome woman. She held nothing back. Whatever was on her mind flowed through her lips as rapid as a firing machine gun. I often wondered how so many words came out so fast. She loved her family, two daughters and a son, the same way. She married, lived in Chester, and has three generations of children.

Uncle Arnold O. ("Junny"), the oldest boy of the thirteen, always had a personal story, doing something that outdid someone else. He was an avid golfer and a western movie fan. He lived at and near the home place most of his life. He married Geraldine Sturdivan, who passed away young, and had one daughter and two sons. He met Sarah Howard, who had twin daughters. His legacy extends unto links of three generations.

Aunt Gracie, the diligent, queenly giver, freely gives of herself and takes time out to check on family routinely since retiring farm life. She married Herbert Bond and lived in

Jarrettsville, successfully rearing her sister's daughter as her own.

Aunt Dorothy A. ("Dottie") is a soul woman who keeps things together. Food and cookouts can spring from out of nowhere around her. She is all about family gatherings and married Morris Hall. They had no children together, but she has raised and supported stepchildren, nieces, and nephews with whatever they may have need of. Yours truly is included, for sure.

Uncle Eugene ("Sonny"), "You can count on me." It amazes me that he can do so much for so many people whenever they call him. When he is not working on someone's house or vehicle, he will fish and cook outside. I love to hear family stories he will tell. He married Grace Lewis, my mom's sister. There are three sons to their legacy, with two extended generations and many others who would like to claim them.

Uncle Paul, "the hard worker," and my dad were very close. He could build and fix a car with great expertise. When I would ask about him, my father would not say much. I found in a newspaper dated April 20, 1956:

> Youth Dies in Crash, Havre de Grace, Maryland
> Paul Spencer Bishop, 18-year-old Negro of near Havre de Grace, was instantly killed early today when his car collided head-on with a septic tank truck near here.

My father, George Wesley Bishop, married my mom, Anne Lewis, having three children, two sons and a daughter, with two generations extending their legacy. He has another son born before they ever met, with grandfather status, continues my father's legacy, generations to three tiers. "I'm a great-uncle!"

Uncle Albert is the "worldly traveler." I was too young to remember my first encounter with him. I do recall the many phone calls my father would receive from him. There was a lot I heard of my uncle Albert, and it was not until I was eighteen that I actually met him. We have interesting conversations about him being a pastor and a policeman, traveling various places, and living in California. He married and divorced Martha after having two daughters, extending his legacy two generations. He has another son and daughter and cared for others.

Uncle Ronald ("Butch") is the busy builder. I recall my teacher, architect, entrepreneur, and construction-worker uncle always building on something, with the majority of the work occurring at the same time. I often wonder if he ever slept. He married Arthurine Nixon, a wonderful supportive wife. They have an admirable son and adopted twin daughters, who are like big sisters to me, and another son and daughter. The family links extend three generations of this couple's legacy

Hortence Irene passed on as an infant. She was born in August 1944 and died June 18, 1945.

My gratitude, appreciation, and great affection for my aunts and uncles extend well beyond words. The togetherness shown throughout the years has been impressive. It was unparalleled and without doubt unpredictable in its makeup. I have been in awe with my family. Its many differences in personality, lifestyle, and living locations were remarkable. Collectively, either by phone or in gathering together, they avoid anarchy for the sake of the overall family. The impression upon me is life-giving, whether my uncles and aunts realize or not. Their lives individually, as well as collectively, have been an inspiration and a comfort to me and many.

I wish time could be turned back on the present generation in a way so they too could experience God-inspired family closeness as past generations did. I know God had designed and ordained the Bishop-Bond family despite life's discouraging ups and downs. He knows all about and has control over all situations. My family has guided me to believing, and I can testify. I can depend on God. There is great joy in knowing where I came from, and I can still return to the home place.

In August 1964, my mother and father married and, for a period of time, lived with Pop-Pop and Mom-Mom at the home place. I was born and brought home to this nurturing center to live with my parents and grandparents, surrounded by aunts, uncles, cousins, and great-uncles and great-aunts as well. One story told is that my grandparents would kidnap me from my baby crib for morning strolls and parade me up and down the road as my parents remained sleeping in bed.

My father and mother met when his older brother and her older sister married eight years earlier. Neither one thought anything of each other then. He went in the military service. She finished high school. Years later, the old brother's gospel group traveled while singing. My mother joined her older sister, and my parents met and remained together until my father's death in 1995. My father was a hardworking man who turned his dream and love for tractor-trailers into a bad business.

My parents always consistently worked hard. Dad handled heavy equipment in street maintenance, and my mother drove school buses and worked in canning house factories during the summer season peeling tomatoes and shucking corn. In the 1980s, I was grown; I graduated from high school and worked at and learned to manage an eatery called George's Chicken House. People often wrongly thought it was my father's store, that being his name. My father had absolutely no interest in dealing with food, other than hauling it. I was a store manager before I was seventeen, and I worked double time while attending college full time.

During that summer, the owners opened a new store in Aberdeen, and I was responsible for training almost everyone. This store was huge and included breakfast. I worked most of the day there and then in the original store at night with no days off. I had no thought of my diabetes other than taking the one shot in the morning, and that was it. On my birthday, I asked off, but I did not even remember my birthday. I had crashed in bed the entire night and the following day. I woke up and said good morning to my dad.

He said, "It is nighttime."

It seems typical of the members of my family that we will work without realizing how hard. We will go until we are physically unable to go anymore. With this stubborn spirit, I developed insomnia and diabetes complications, and work became my social life. I had no other goals or ideas at the time of doing anything else. My mind was set on what I was doing.

My dad dreamed of owning his own business. His mind was set on driving tractor-trailers and turning it into business. He cashed in all his pension stocks from BGE and purchased several trucks. My father worked during the day and drove during the night. He hired other men to drive the other trucks while maintenance and upkeep kept him down-spiraling into deeper debt.

Over a span of ten years, he had taken out huge secret loans but could not pay them. He was driven to run these trucks but had no business plan in mind. My stubborn father, the dreamer, insisted on achieving his dream of owning a bunch of trucks. I was going to college as an accounting major. The on-hand family endeavor would have been great for me, if I had known. My youth and vitality loved a good challenge. I saw the many trucks and thought they belonged to some guy my father always mentioned in Pennsylvania. I was kept completely in the blind about his business venture. Before we even knew it, a foreclosure sign was on our door. My mom was devastated. I was thunderstruck, and my father was oblivious; somehow he went and purchased a charter bus.

Our home was no longer our home. The house where my mother and father nurtured three children and a host of community and friends was gone, sold at a public sale. We were detached from the only home we knew. I was no longer a child, but it felt as if someone had taken my most cherished marble and best friend from me and cast them into the river. The disconnection from the home, community, and friends left me traumatized. In a daze, I moved to Baltimore with my father's sister.

With little funds, Mom stayed at a motel with my sister. My father and brother stayed out in the trucks. My father did everything within his power to pull our family back together. He begged for a place to stay from a landlord with a reputation of having homes barely fit to live in. Mom reluctantly moved in. That did not last long because my parents could not pay the rent.

My sister joined the armed services. I remained in Baltimore. My brother was with friends and then got locked up in the county jail. My mom stayed with her brother. My father stayed with his trucks at the home place. The house had collapsed on itself years earlier, and my father turned the property into a junkyard of tires, old cars, trucks, and pieces of scrap metal. I was not sure what the other members of the family thought, but I was beside myself, not able to understand my father's stubborn obsession. I know my "Big Pop-Pop," my father's father, would not have allowed such a mess.

A FIRM FAMILY
FELLOWSHIP

My family, like many others, has its ups and downs. We are located all across the country. Interwoven within the confines of time and history, I live among a modest community, a group of ordinary people who live for those around them. Although disconnected by miles and by years of living busy lives, when we all come together—what an omnipotent force of a feeling, something indescribable that only God has ordained. As part of this force that made me who I am, I have researched deeply into its roots.

When I started seriously looking in the roots of my family, I naively assumed all people with the surname Bishop were related. I began to realize the enormous number of people in Maryland alone with that same family name. Instead of looking at that vast picture, I started with the little pieces connected with my close family, myself, and my grandfather.

In August 1979, I remember my mother, father, and aunts preparing for a bus trip to Atlanta, Georgia. My parents rarely went away or out anywhere. I do not believe they even had a honeymoon. This trip was exceptional because my father's sister had planned this much-awaited trip. Cousins were set to watch younger siblings, and all was in order when my father received a very late phone call the night before departure. Pop had died. His father, my grandfather, the father of thirteen children, had passed on at age eighty years old. As a teenager, I often went to bed late, and this night I happened to be there for my father. I did not say anything but thought the trip was off. My parents deserved this long-anticipated trip as much as anyone else, and I was looking forward to them going, even without me, my brother, and my sister. I was looking forward to cousins looking after me anyway, even though most of the time I ended up looking after myself and taking care of them. To my surprise, my father said they were going anyway, and off they went.

The earliest record of my grandfather I found was in the federal census record of 1900. He is listed as Oscar, born March 1899 in the household of his father, Augustus Bishop, and mother, Celesta, on Ostego Street in the town of Havre de Grace, Maryland. As I remember, Big Pop-Pop didn't say much. He would offer me butterscotch candy and crunchy peanut brittle. When we visited, he seemed to always be sitting at the kitchen table and looking out the window, gazing out through the old apple and pear trees to the yard where my father would work on cars and trucks. He would be sitting there at a table with an ashtray of cigarette butts and bottles of booze—Old Grand-Dad, Jack Daniel's, and others—as the radio in the background broadcasted a ball game.

As I remember, he was a tall, well-built, slender man with a bald head and a funny-looking eye. His voice was deep and strong. I had never heard him ever raise his voice, but others said he was a mean man and that they trembled when he spoke loudly. Thinking back, I can only imagine someone touching a wrong nerve with him and getting cussed out. I suppose his later years resolved him not saying too much around us grandchildren. But to me, he was my Big Pop-Pop, a gentle, loving giant of a man with a bass voice. To the grandchildren, no matter how much we wanted to run around the yard and play when we visited, instinctively we knew to greet and speak to our Pop-Pop. Something was said by someone if it was not done. Even to this day when going by the home place, even though the house is gone, within me lingers a sense of respect and a lasting impression not erased by fading memory but embedded by the bequest within my being. I am intrigued by the confident sense of strength, resilience, and silent security my grandfather had. Even with rather vague memories of Pop-Pop, remnants of his traits connect within my being and many generations.

One day my dad was driving my grandfather to Baltimore City to stay with my father's sister. Dad loved Chevy vehicles. During his lifetime, he owned, fixed up, and pieced together many. On this fall day, he had picked-up Pop-Pop with my brother and me sitting in the backseat, ready to ride. My mischievous little brother was up to no good.

Earlier that day, being the nature buff that I am, I had picked some cattail pods. I wanted to try to grow the brown, slender, tube-shaped marsh plant from the seeds. Well, my brother would not leave them alone on the backseat floor. I guess he wanted to get me in trouble by getting a response from my grandfather, who sat in the seat directly in front of me. My brother took the end of the cattail and hit the back of Pop-Pop's bald head, smirking. I had closed my eyes, expecting words or something to fly over the seat.

The next thing I knew, the car was pulling over as we were crouched on the back floor trying to hide. I knew he had done it now. The car door opened, then closed, and there was silence as I arose to see what was going on. I thought, *We in trouble now.* As I looked through the car's front window, I saw my father walking into the store alone. Pop-Pop Bishop was still silent and looking out the window. My brother looked at me and shrugged his shoulders.

My father had stopped at a liquor store to get something for Pop-Pop. My dad neither drank nor smoked, and to see us stopping at this store was surprising to me. With a brown paper bag, Dad got back in the car and sat the bag next to my grandfather. My brother and I snickered and giggled, and he asked, "What are you two up to?"

I was relieved to have escaped wrath, and we both started laughing. I smacked my brother with the cattail, and it burst open with the white, furry, feathery seeds flying everywhere. We continued to my aunt's house with a trail of cattail seeds flying out the window. Dad mentioned something about snow flurries to my grandfather. Pop-Pop looked around but never said a word the whole time. I laughed so hard that my stomach hurt the entire way. To this day, I have never tried to grow any cattails.

Growing up, Pop-Pop and his siblings were surrounded by family in Havre de Grace. Both born and raised within this small town, his father and mother's family history are well rooted in this village that was later known as a city. I can imagine him and his cousins walking the narrow horse-buggy alleys and streets alongside roaming chickens, ducks, and hogs. Other relatives worked as coal heavers for the railroad trains and boat ferries as people moved through this major travel town to cross the river to Philadelphia. I think about uncles fishing nearby and aunts making sure the children get off to the school or social hall. This small community in the early 1900s was regarded as a city because of the constant flow of travelers following the main route between D.C. and New York City. Those living and residing within the city were close and undoubtedly knew one another, especially in the African American community.

My grandfather attended school at the Anderson Institute at the corner of Ontario and Stokes Street, where his father served on the board. As a teenager, he helped his father at the local lumberyard and worked with relatives at various day-labor carpenter jobs. As a family, Pop-Pop, his siblings, and both parents lived in the city of Havre de Grace until sometime between 1915 and 1917; then they all moved to Philadelphia, Pennsylvania. As I think about those times, I can just imagine my grandfather being torn between leaving the people, places, and things he knew and the thrill of moving to a big city like Philadelphia.

As a teenager, my Pop-Pop became involved in packing and taking care of things while helping move seven younger siblings with his parents. How did they travel? There were very few motorized cars at that time, even though they were increasingly in demand. The boat was not as popular as the steam trains and horse-drawn carriages at that time. Today in my car, it takes me a little over an hour to get to Philly. However, the family moved, possibly traveling all at once or gradually with a few family members and things at a time, over a period of time. It had to have been quite an all-day trip, traveling about sixty-five miles from Havre de Grace, Maryland, to the city of Philadelphia.

At the time of the move, great national changes were occurring. The twentieth century was new. The generation of hard-timers arrived at the peak of the industrial boom. War was in foreign countries, and immigrants inundated America. The sense of improvement for all was in the air. The nation was rapidly moving, with people in rural areas pursuing opportunities in big cities and factories producing in assembly lines. Women won the right to vote. Societies were organized to promote social reform. W. E. B. Dubois, Marcus Garvey, Mary Bethune-McCloud, and others embraced and promoted a spirit of equality and unity for all, especially advocating for African Americans. My grandfather was in the midst of it all, connecting generation to generation.

The Great War broke out in Europe, and in 1917, America was thrown into World War I. I found the WWI draft cards for my grandfather and his father. On September 12, 1918, they both reported to the thirty-fifth draft-board station to register.

Written on Pop-Pop's registration card was:

> Oscar J. Bishop, 2055 Pierce St., Phila, Pa. age 19,
> born March 31, 1899, Negro(√), native born (√),
> Laborer, Drehmann Paving Co., 2622 Parrish St.
> Phila, Pa, nearest relative-Celesta Bishop, 2055
> Pierce St. Phila. Pa.
> Signed: Oscar Bishop

On the back of this card was:

> Height-tall (√), Build-medium (√), color of eyes-
> Dark, color of hair-Black

Comments: Lost sight of right eye
Dated signed by James J. Parker
Stamped with the board address

This was the first time I learned that my grandfather had little sight in that funny-looking right eye. However, here it was, written out and signed. I had not heard of family members ever speaking of it, and no one seemed to ask about it until now. So it is said, by one of his children, that Pop-Pop's eye injury occurred when he was a child, from a spiny nut burr that had fallen from a chestnut tree. Another child said he was injured during a fight over a girl. To me, that is hard to believe because I would not think he would let anyone get the best of him. Possibly, it was a combination of both or none at all. He became who he was through the circumstances life revealed to him. Life is not ever picture-perfect. Evidently, my grandfather pressed on in spite of his eye to work, live, and raise a family with many generations.

What comes to my mind is my strong, youthful grandfather working long, hard days mixing and layering asphalt on busy streets and raising buildings of this ever-growing city of Philadelphia, Pennsylvania, during the early part of the twentieth century. As an inexperienced man from a small city, the allure of new cultures and activities surely piqued his curiosity. I could image the speakeasies, gangsters, bootleggers, socialites, and the like.

The 1920 federal census lists my Bishop family living on Pierce Street in Philadelphia, Pennsylvania. My grandfather Oscar is listed as a laborer in a factory. Upon looking up several addresses from the census, I discovered that other relatives from Harford County, Maryland, moved to the same neighborhood. Did they know? Was the community bond that strong? Whatever the relationship, they arose to the opportunity together to face the change and challenge of the transition from rural living into the city. I discovered that this particular neighborhood was comprised of clusters of two-story tenant houses. In 1922, these houses were torn down to build blocks of three-story row homes, which we see today.

It is amazing to me that so many people can live in close-quartered areas in such a city. When I lived in Baltimore with my aunt, the row home seemed horribly boxed in. I was so sensitive to hearing neighbors move on both sides of the wall. Living in the city took time for me to adjust to. I had to tune out the sound of the people constantly walking and vehicles moving. Many families had to do what they could do to provide for one another. Today that sense of community and closeness is rapidly vanishing. Whether by coincidence or knowingly, two Harford County families were just a few blocks from each other in the big city in the 1920s.

At the corner of Ninth and Locust Street lived Raymond, Josephine, and their four-year-old son, William Hilton. Josephine's sisters often visited from Maryland. Relatives and close community friends often moved in and lived near one another in other cities. I believe my grandfather knew them from childhood. The Hilton couples were the same age as my grandfather. In general, the African American community was tightly linked. I can't help but wonder about social gatherings or events that led to bringing this family to the attention of Oscar, my grandfather. Ultimately, as these families traveled back and forth to Maryland, my grandfather became married to Sarah A. Bond, the younger sister of Josephine. The young couple, after living a few years in the big city, moved back to Maryland to a small village outside Havre de Grace called Gravel Hill, surrounded by the fellowship of close family and friends.

Great Bishop Siblings

A sense of connection to people, even family, is not a constant. I see how this present generation detaches itself from people and relies more on superficial communications rather than personal connectedness. I think social networking via computer is fine in moderation, like most things. My mind, body, and spirit need that natural, physical interaction to vibe the human soul. Let me connect eye-to-eye with the true you. I relate better through personal conversation and finding commonality and confirmation of the spirit within a person. In many cases, we know who we can connect with during our first personal contact. Special bonds develop through ongoing social interactions among one another. I realize I do not connect with everyone at the same depth. I believe the spirit within us draws us to particular people at a certain time for a specific purpose. The dynamics of family are different throughout; some are disconnected, and many are very close.

I realize, even though there are many high-tech devices to stay connected with each other, we have been overloaded with innovative distractions that threaten our individuality within the family. In my opinion, connection that becomes family legacy is the act of passing positive attributes along for the advancement of the whole. I am part of the Bishop-Bond legacy. Already my selfless contributions to share, encourage, and inspire through what was passed to me, whether I know it or not, has become my legacy.

Growing up, I admired the closeness and bond among my father's siblings. Despite miles between most of them, they were connected. They knew who was where and how each one was doing almost daily. It was an interwoven network of communication via phone and visits to each other's homes on a regular basis. I was amazed in how instinctive the system was, even when I tried to interject. A prime example was seeing a cousin in a store one day who let me know another cousin unexpectedly was in town. His family was trying to have a little cookout. Since we had not seen the visiting cousin in years, I went home to tell my dad, knowing he had other plans. But a brother had stopped by, and his sisters had already called. My good news had already been superseded by their link.

I am convinced my grandfather influenced his children's closeness. He had left all his siblings in Philadelphia and moved back to Maryland. Whether by tradition or as deliberate signs of the family's closeness, generations after generations are named after one another. This is very much so with my grandfather and his siblings and their children. Many times it would be quite confusing who was talking about whom. Throughout the years, many attempts of reconnecting occurred. "Pop Oscar" traveled when he could financially. I believe many letters had been written before getting a phone. I was told the home place was one of the first to get a phone when it became available in the area. I noticed Pop Oscar's sister was an operator in the 1930 census. She could have influenced the installation of the phone.

I vaguely remember a reunion in the '70s when Pop-Pop Oscar's sister and brothers came down from the northern states of New York and Pennsylvania. One photo triggers memories. I remember playing among many cousins in my uncle Butch's yard. The older cousins were around a volleyball net, and there were many chairs scattered around the tables throughout the grassy field. This was the first family reunion that I believe the Bishop-Bonds held. The only picture I saw of this grand family gathering was of my grandfather sitting next to his sister Gracie and brother Arnold. I vividly remember my great-aunt Gracie being a very emotional woman. I rarely saw so many tears. I think it was my mom who said Aunt Gracie was overly happy to be with her brothers all together with many generations.

I want to also honor and pay tribute to the lives of my great-aunt and great-uncles and their families. Their accomplishments, I hear, range from being the first professional athlete in the area to holding high-level positions serving country and community. This legacy of Augustus Bishop and Celesta Durbin-Bishop connects generation to generation. These are the nine children of this couple:

My grandfather, Oscar Jerome Bishop, Born March 31, 1899, he married Sarah Amelia Bond in 1922 and had thirteen children. He resided in Maryland until his death in August 1979.

Mary Bishop was born in April 1900 and died as an infant in about 1901.

Grace Virginia Bishop was born June 7, 1901. She married Joseph Gay; they had no children. She lived in Elmont, New York, until her death in June 1980.

Eugene Bishop was born in July 1903 and died in December 1980.

Albert Bently Bishop, born December 1, 1904, married Caroline Langston in 1929, and they had two sons together.

He resided in Philadelphia, Pennsylvania until his death on November 8, 1998, with a legacy of generations.

Lawrence Bishop was born about 1908. Research is ongoing.

Kenneth Carol Bishop was born in 1909. He married Catherine Parrant. Their union born three sons; one died as a toddler. He lived in Philadelphia until his death on November 11, 1959.

William Arnold Bishop was born on January 11, 1911. He married Pauline Irby and had two daughters. He died in Camden, New Jersey, on September 22, 1999.

Elmer Frederick Bishop was born on February 14, 1914. He married Hauzie Monroe Johnson in 1938 and had two sons. He lived in Brooklyn, New York, at his death on April 1, 1973.

At every reunion since the '70s, I have gradually gotten to know my cousins from Philadelphia, New York, and beyond. We do not see each other often; it seems we do only when a reunion occurs. I know family when we do connect; many times we end up speaking for hours. I love my family, even to the third, fourth, or more cousin tier.

Mom Sarah Bond-Bishop

On March 30, 1922, a day before his twenty-third birthday, Pop Oscar Bishop married Mom Sarah Bond in Elkton, Cecil County, Maryland. The license states both were residents of Philadelphia, Pennsylvania. This union began the Bishop-Bond family. What a gift, creating a united legacy with lasting remnants of the united bond and connection of bonds that extend to many generations! This prolific union was by God's ordained design.

The first known record of my grandmother is in the 1910 federal census. She is listed as Sarah A., age eight years old, fifth child of seven children of George W. and Amelia A. Bond. Her family reside within three to four miles northwest of the city of Havre de Grace, Maryland, near Hopewell and a freedmen's village called Gravelly Hills. "Mom-Mom Sarah" grew up in the meadows of the area surrounded by farms and woodland. I can imagine her following after her older brothers and sisters. Within this area, her mother was born and raised among many family members. Her father, although born in Peach Bottom, Pennsylvania, was raised nearby also. My grandmother was nurtured by loving parents and older siblings, as well as relatives and friends of the families.

She went to a one-room schoolhouse for African American children within the nearby small community. Mom-Mom Sarah, with her siblings and cousins, was taught the basics in education: reading, writing, and arithmetic. A select few with the collective sacrifice of the community were sent away for higher learning. Advanced education was rather expensive for African American people; a home domestic was the main vocation of women during these times. Despite the advocacy of equal women's rights in the big cities, rural life was laid back and withdrawn from the active change that was occurring in urban areas.

When the Great War began in 1917, I can imagine her teenage concerns as military recruiters and draft boards canvassed the areas for young people to serve. Her brothers and cousins were at the right age of enlistment. With the promise of good wages and opportunities the military offered, was it possible she entertained the idea of service?

During those times, African Americans, not to mention women, seldom enjoyed the same chances afforded white males. Society then was reluctant to accept the abilities and great potential exhibited by women and men of color.

As the Great War, later known as World War I, progressed, the older brother and cousins served overseas. Mom-Mom Sarah's family moved to Perryville across the river in Cecil County, Maryland. They lived near the public health center now known as Perrypoint Veterans Hospital. My grandmother's family was one of the first black families to work at the center. I discovered in the 1920 census that my grandmother was listed with her family at age seventeen as a servant in the public health hospital's commissary.

Initially, the US Public Health Service opened at Perrypoint; its facility functioned as a general hospital that provided care for patients with various disabilities. The Bond family helped with the building and main maintenance upkeep. In 1920, the US Public Health Hospital in Cape May, New Jersey, closed, and patients were transferred to Perrypoint, and four more of the buildings in the village were converted for hospital use. It was at this time that Perrypoint became a hospital that focused on neuropsychiatric care. The US Veterans Bureau took over on May 1, 1922, and the facility is known as the Perrypoint VA Hospital to this day.

My grandmother's family made a major contribution in the advancement of this facility into recent decades. As her family served, worked, and built a working village, Mom-Mom Sarah made visits to Philly to help her sister Josephine. Family members say that Great-Aunt Josephine's child at birth weighed over ten pounds, and she vowed not to have any more children. I can imagine her sisters being there throughout this very difficult pregnancy. Billie, her only child born, married a foreign woman, Tomi, in Merced, California. In 1987, he died at age seventy-two, with no known children.

Also living in Philly on Locust Street was my grand-mother's cousin, Ida Harris-Phillips (Snead). In 1920, she was recently widowed, and she started a lucrative catering service. My grandmother Mom-Mom Sarah and her new husband, Oscar, moved in with them as time roared into the 1920s.

The era after World War I was a time of great prosperity for our country. The working American had to adapt to the ever-changing industrial growth. Factories began using conveyor belts and machines. The workforce that had produced warfare necessities changed to mass-produced consumer items. The radio connected the nation as an increasingly popular item every home could afford to have. Broadcasting stations provided Americans with sermons, news, sports, music, and commentaries of the day. Airwaves connected all to impute opinion, set trends, and unite a popular national voice, whether right or wrong, for the majority. I can imagine my young grandmother spending hours listening to a radio in her sister's and cousins' homes.

The '20s, for many people, was a happy period. It was an era of good times to forget the anxiousness of the future and pains of the past era and set the framework for our modern age with fresh ideas, newfangled inventions, and new ways. The popularity of jazz music spread with recordings and radio and big-band performances. Silent films presented visuals of comedians and dramatic movie shows, which brought attention to fashion for men and women.

I can imagine my grandmother Sarah as a young adult, experiencing the sound of her first radio broadcast or seeing her initial silent movie and Broadway show. Perhaps Mom-Mom Sarah adorned a beaded flapper dress with accessories and a fur shawl to cover her shoulders. She could have straightened her hair with Madame C. J. Walker's newly designed hair comb for a bobbed hairstyle. I can imagine her dancing to the upbeat jazz music or even sitting, looking beautiful, by the stage of Duke Ellington's big band. Maybe she just watched quietly, working in the background. Either way, my grandmother, impressionable and young in the midst of it all, was connecting generation to generation.

Mom-Mom Sarah was nineteen years old when she and Pop-Pop Oscar united in holy matrimony in March 1922. Time has concealed the specific events of their living situation and wedding. They lived in Philly during the early years of married life and started a family. In 1927, my grandparents moved into her grandfather's home on Gravel Hill Road in Havre de Grace, Maryland. Here they and their toddler daughters began life anew in a slow, safe environment established as the family home place.

Great Bond Siblings

As I remember my grandmother's siblings, I get good feelings; they were all extremely nice. The home place would not have been what it was without them. Their generosity, kind hearts, and peaceful spirits invariably made a person happy. Mom-Mom Sarah was the sixth child of eight born to George W. and Amelia A. Harris-Bond. Her mother,

Amelia, grew-up at the "home place," and they all lived on Gravel Hill at one point or another.

Aunt Josephine Bond was born on November 23, 1890, and she married Wm. Raymond Hilton from Hopewell. They had one son, Billie, who married Tomi but had no children. Aunt Josephine loved hugs. Late in life, she developed complications with diabetes, became blind, and required a double amputation. She could make you laugh so hard at the things she would say. She died in September 1977.

Alexander Franklin Bond was born in July 1892 and died on August 28, 1903.

Uncle Harry Filmore Bond was born on September 14, 1893, married Ellen Elizabeth Stokes, who died on September 24, 1924. Then he married Eliza C. Taylor on October 18, 1928, and they had eleven children with several tiers of generations. He died on June 11, 1990.

Aunt "Stella" Estella Christina Bond was born on August 16, 1896, and she married James R. Jones; she had four daughters with several tiers of generations. She raised many foster children. She died on November 3, 1983.

Uncle George Henderson was born on October 18, 1899, and he married Marie Tildon. They adopted a daughter. He died on May 16, 1976.

Mom-Mom Sarah Amelia Bond was born on November 28, 1902, and she married Oscar J. Bishop and had thirteen children. She died on January 14, 1966.

Aunt Lucy Alberta Bond was born on June 27, 1906. She never married and had no children. She raised my cousin as her own. She died on November 9, 1991.

Uncle Charles Wesley Bond was born on August 28, 1910. He married Mary Sallie. They did not have children together but adopted. He died on July 31, 1977.

My great-aunts and great-uncles hold a special spot in my heart. They stayed close together to the very end. They always knew what one another were doing. They made their family the community, and many neighbors, even those not blood-related, became part of this Bond family. These brothers and sisters exemplified the practice of praying together and staying together. They did many things together residing on Gravel Hill and having homes near each other. Participating in church functions and the community was the center of their life. My sister remembers and reflects on the family:

> Growing up in the seventies and eighties were remarkable and memorable times. Being the third child born to the late George W. Bishop and Anne L. Bishop, the only girl, I remember the summers spent at the "home place," which is finally known as Gravel Hill Road. There, my brothers Reggie, Reesie, and I would go around the entire neighbor all day, playing with all the Gravel Hill kids. Of course, with our curiosity, we did things that we weren't supposed to do, like swimming in the gravel pits and walking through the woods. Our mother was surely mad when she saw us swimming in the gravel pit. In addition, during our times spent at Gravel Hill, our father would take us to visit with the various relatives who lived out there. I remember going to the house of Aunts Lucy and Stella Bond, big Mom-Mom's (Sarah Bishop's) sisters. At first, the big, dark two-story house scared me, but when I met them, their gentle, sweet spirits eased my fear. It

was very good to have met them, because they were a nice reflection of a grandmother I never had the opportunity to meet.

Back then, Aunt Lucy was our church's pianist. Playing the piano has been a God-given talent throughout the generations between the Bishop and Bond families. Cousin Lindsay Bond, who played the piano also, could play with the smoothest jazz sound I've ever heard. I as well play the piano but could never compare to the great musicians in our family who were before me. What a rich and rewarding legacy that has been stored into our two families. I only pray that the Bishop and Bond legacies will live with my children, Tyrissa and Brandon, and their children and their children's children.

I often remember in church that Uncle Harry could pray the walls down if he wanted to. I believe Aunts Stella's verbal calls and responses with loud, "Yes, Lords" and "Amens" kept him praying even more fervently. Aunt Lucy played the piano so hard that you'd think the whole neighborhood needed to hear her. Uncle George also played the piano regularly at a sister church. Other family members kept watch in unison as ushers at the door, whoever was near could not help but join in praising God.

I remember at fifteen I was very excited about working at a sub shop, but they laid me off. They actually let me go for being so slow. Well, I was disappointed. My great-aunt Stella instinctively knew something was wrong; she was looking at me intently until she could get close enough to ask if I was okay and what was wrong. I told her about the job, and she said it would be all right and I would get another. She always had encouraging words. That summer I went back and got another job at the eatery. I became the store manager. That lasted three years.

My great-aunt Lucy was a hugger like her older sister. She was the sensitive one. I dared not pass her by without speaking and giving her a hug. She would tell the rest of the family, and I would not know what had happened, especially when I was distracted from giving her my attention. Below are some written notes from a small, worn, and torn white Bible:

Presented to Mother Estella C. Jones
by daughter Dorothy and son-in-law
Paul Spencer, Mother's Day, May 1956

Aug. 23, 1959, a.m. Sunday
Beautiful and cold, will warm up later

While sitting here, these thoughts come to me. This is my sermon, no more—no less.

I am nearing my God to thee. We are standing at the crossroad, some looking for work, others looking for pleasure, others for peace. But I am looking neither to the right nor left, but straight ahead. I intend to walk and walk, run a little and not worrie (weary) until I come to the long, white-stoned steps. I shall start to my climb, to climb and climb. Take my time that I don't miss a step. I will feel myself getting tired, but I will continue to climb as my shoulder begins to stiff and my breath is getting short. I look, and just beyond the steps is a tiny light.

I feel I am nearing the landing, and then I feel as though I stepped out on a carpet trimmed in gold. My feet do not seem to touch the floor as I continue to walk. There is a beautiful gate just ahead; it begins to slowly open. My father is standing to one side, my mother to the other, saying, "Welcome, child, come on home and take your rest." Then I look, and there is a greater light. This light is Jesus beckoning me to come in. Then there's singing, softly and tenderly. Jesus is calling, "Come home, come home."

Dedicated to:
My three daughters—Dorothy, Helen, and Hazel
My three sisters—Josephine, Sarah, and Lucy
My three brothers—Harry, George, and Charles
My sons-in-law—Paul, Howard, Dickie, Charles (Melvin Mills)
My grandchildren—Paul Jr., Melvin, Charles, Richard, Darnell, Thomasina, Gary, Diann Lee Chaylesa Mills
I did my best for all, been here, shed blood and many tears, but this day I ask God to wipe away all tears. I am old now, sixty-three years.
Signed by Estella Bond Jones

Hazel went to work at the Officer's Club Aberdeen Proving Grounds in July 1963.

Spent my vacation with Paul, Dot, and Melvin in Camden, New Jersey, from the 6th of August to the 18th of August. Richard brought me home at evening time.

Helen, Charles, and children came on here from Harvey, Illinois, and arrived here August 11, 1963, and returning the 23rd.

Arrived in Vineyard Haven on Saturday, August 17, 1968, with the Jays. I am now seventy-two years old, have the same sermon, but others added. I have twelve grandchildren, two great-grandchildren. Leaving Vineyard Haven on September 3, 1968, for Camden, New Jersey.

Cousin Virginia passed away September 1969.
Hugh Branford passed away September 1969.

Highway to heaven
I am walking up the King's highway

The Lord's Prayer
6th Chapter of St. Matthew, 9th verse
"After this manner therefore pray ye: Our Father which art in heaven, hallowed be thy name."

I shall not be moved
Just like a tree planted by the waters

Judges 2:4-8

IN GOD'S SERVICE

I am captivated by the Bishop and Bond family in the way they unite and come together to do things. It is a legacy, their way of life, and a dedicated testimony to others. My uncle tells me of the gospel quartet group called The Silvertones, formed by my grandfather Oscar Bishop, great-uncles Harry Bond and George Bond, and cousin Leon Bond. My uncle Sonny was inspired with Ike and Paul Taylor, Earl, Kurt, and Vernon Jones to sing as the Sensational Silvertones. They traveled throughout the East Coast singing gospel songs representing their home church, St. James AME Gravel Hill. The family also helped organize several groups within the church. The United Ushers was a group of ushers from various churches and denominations from all over the state. My grandmother Sarah, her sister Stella, and others of the present generations served as "doorkeepers in the house of the Lord." As mentioned, this family loves music. If a family member did not have a musical instrument in hand or at their fingertips, they used their voice as an instrument for song. Ironically, a document dated in the late 1700s states my several-great-grandfather Harry Bond played violin. Is it through links in kinship or the consistent traditional training? Whatever the reason, a natural family talent for music across generations helped increase family ties.

The sense of community and coming together has been a theme throughout for the Bishop-Bond family. The center of this connection was both the home and the church. Many activities, events, and memories have occurred in the more than 160-year existence of the now St. James AME Church. Many family members became ordained leaders and ministers in the church. In 1990, I too was ordained an itinerant minister. Growing up among family in the church was normal for me, whereas my research revealed a surprise not even the eldest member in the family had known or heard of.

My search began when my uncle said as a youngster he remembers vividly the carrying of a coffin. My grandfather and several uncles would carry a coffin by hand from Chapel Road deep into the wooded area behind cousin Madelyn's brick home. It was said to be an old family cemetery and the site of the original church, St. James. I decided to investigate. I recruited my uncle Butch, who had a huge machete blade to cut the overgrown thicket, and neighborhood friends the Jonases. I did not know what I would discover.

Once we cleared through the overgrowth of the edge thickets, it cleared to a hilly ravine that bottomed by a dry streambed. The trees were huge, and the area seemed not to have seen human activity for almost a century. The trees had left a thick blanket of coverings throughout the vast area. We searched for hours and for what seemed like square miles to find anything. Under some fallen trees, I saw what looked like remnants of a foundation. It could have been the church. Not far from the foundation and obviously out of place was a boulder that was five feet high and three feet wide. As I touched the rock and cleared vines, my imagination overloaded a picture of free people of color and slaves all meeting at the rock.

We searched until we could physically search no more. As we sluggishly came out of the thickets, a man greeted us and asked what we were looking for.

We replied, "An old cemetery."

"It is at the edge of my yard," he said with enthusiasm.

The man eagerly walked us to it. The cemetery could be seen through the trees just off the yard's edge, and farther into the wooded area were even more stones of various shapes and sizes. Sunken grave plots and the ground covered in vinca vines was a perfect resting place of peace, with occasional interruptions from a railroad train's horn in the background. My friends started to write the names down off the tombstones we could read, the majority being members of the Skinner family, my grandfather's mother's family, and, from the Civil War, Sergeant James Hill, United States Colored Troops.

This land once belonged to my family. My grandfather Oscar Bishop's mother was Celesta Durbin, named after her aunt and grandmother Celesta Skinner, who married Stephen Durbin. My research is still ongoing, even though I have collected a good bit of information on the Durbin and Skinner families. While investigating additional family members to find leads to my grandfather's mother's vital information, I discovered an interesting history. I have not located my grandfather's mother's death certificate, but I located other Durbin family members in the process.

In the 1900 census, Jane Durbin, born in March 1837, was listed in Pop Augustus and Mom Celesta Bishop's household as a sixty-three-year-old, single grandmother.

Her death certificate, dated May 8, 1910, indicates she was seventy-four years of age, single, and born to father Bonaparte Durbin and a mother unknown. Her son Thomas Durbin signed the form. The 1880 census lists Jane Durban with son Thomas, twenty-five; William, five; Frank, three; and daughters Mary, sixteen, and Eliza, nine. In 1863, Dr. John Sappington, near Chapel Road, in an area which is now an exclusive housing development and golf course, transferred Thomas Scott Durbin, age ten, to Helen Sappington. This was one of the last slave records to have been filed at the courthouse before the Emancipation Proclamation. Ten years earlier, Sappington had filed the following freedom paper:

May 9, 1853

To all whom it may concern, be it known that I, John K. Sappington, of Harford County in the State of Maryland, for diverse goods causes and consideration me there unto moving have released from slavery, liberated, manumitted and set free and by these present do release from slavery, liberate, manumit and set free the following named and described Negroes, said manumission to take effect and be enforced from and after the times here in after mentioned of that is to say Grace Durbin's son, Stephen Durbin, born on the 7th of December 1837, to be free at the age of twenty-eight; Martha Jane Durbin (daughter of Grace Durbin) born on the 9th of March 1836 to be free when twenty-eight years and her issue to be free when twenty-eight years of age; and Anthony Bryant Durbin, son of the said Martha Jane Durbin, born on the 16th

December 1851, to be free when he shall arrive to the age of twenty-eight years.

This freedom paper and the death certificates on both Stephen and Jane (Martha) Durbin mention Bonaparte Durbin as their father, and this document states Grace as mother. Listed on this document are other families named Ramsey, Jackson, and Taylor to be set free. These are all relatives of Celesta Durbin on her grandmother's side.

My grandfather's mother's name, Celesta, was carried from the Skinner side of the family. Stephen Durbin married Celesta Skinner, as noted in land records of a mortgage from John Sappington on the property passed down through to her family off Chapel Road. The area was where the St. James AME Church first originated near James Peaco's home before relocating to Gravel Hill and Green Street within the city of Havre de Grace. The Bishop-Bond family was greatly instrumental in establishing and supporting this church in God's service.

The area off Chapel Road had been home to this family for generations. Horace Skinner and second wife Hattie Martin-Skinner had acquired the land in1846 from her father, Moses Martin (HDG 31/368). I believe Horace, with his siblings, had been enslaved with the Dallam family. In 1823, Henrietta Dallam set free at age thirty years old the following Negroes: Fanny was to be freed in 1846; Amos was to be freed in 1843, service of Thomas Dallam; Horace was to be freed in 1848; and Henry was to be freed in 1853, service of Jas Dallam. On June 27, 1840, Horace married first wife Sydney Martin, the sister of Hattie, at St. John's Episcopal Church in Havre de Grace. Henry Skinner was trustee at St. James AME Church in Gravel Hill in the late 1880s.

In the 1850 and 1860 federal census schedule, Horace Skinner was listed with Hattie and children. Lysta or Celesta A. was about six in the first and was listed with nine other children in the second census. In 1860, there was a fifty-eight-year-old Horace listed as a laborer and a forty-year-old wagon carter with real estate valued at five hundred dollars. In 1865, this land was passed to Celesta and husband, Stephen Durbin (WHD 16/169).

In 1828, Moses Martin and Sally Frances purchased two acres of land from Richard Barnes. Martin purchased two additional lots of more than five acres in 1830 (HD 13/348). The Skinner cemetery is located within this land.

LIBERTY AND HONOR

Researching my family tree based on verbal history had its limits, but the journey to trace unknown family history became limitless with the use of archival materials to trace preceding generations. Years ago I started visiting libraries and historical archives to further my family search. While attending a workshop in the state archives, I was approached by a gentleman who was kin to the famous author Alex Haley. He greeted me with, "Hello, cousin."

I was astonished because I had never seen this person before in my life. He noticed I was perplexed and explained. Obviously, he saw my name badge. The Bishop family, he explained, was on a plantation with and near his relative, Kunta Kinte. I explained that I was just starting my research into my family history and had not traced any out of Harford County yet. My memory of that moment continues to consume me with the desire to seek out all relations.

Working at my office job during the day, I would write out notes on researching family history while searching the Internet. Afterward, I would spend countless hours at night searching through images on microfilm of census schedules at my local library. Each visit I would browse through each page, each line, and make copies of households with the last names of Bishop, Bond, Harris, and Durbin. During days off, I would visit the local courthouse and spend hours on research. At the very first visit, I became so involved searching through old land record indexes, I lost track of time. It was well after business hours when I realized the time and thought for sure I had been locked in the basement alone. When I walked up to the lobby, the clock hand was close to 11 p.m. To my surprise, the security guard, who I had not seen all day, said he knew I was there working. I had a lot of information but little, if any, family connection. Not being deterred, I explored the local historical society. I was not sure if anyone could help. I was determined to find something of my family.

As I entered the Historical Society of Harford County, I was overwhelmed by the mass of material available to me. The old Bel Air post office seemed to burst with books and records of the county's rich heritage. I signed in with the receptionist and inquired about membership. The lady was more than helpful. She showed me the library, the different files, index of the family genealogy records, court records, and archives and the days they were open to public researchers. This day I arrived was a Thursday, the day set aside specifically for family research. I asked for assistance in researching my family. A lady asked the last name I was seeking. I told her the Bishop family, and to my surprise, her surname name was Bishop also. I was surprised because she was not African American, and growing up in Harford County, there were very few families with the last name Bishop.

Different ladies started looking through the filing cabinets. After several minutes, one lady pulled out a manila folder containing thin and fragile papers of various sizes. These old papers were certificates of marriage before the turn of the twentieth century. The lady showed me one certificate at a time, asking if this was my family. I was dumbfounded because I did not know. Each certificate could have been a relative. So I asked for copies of them all. I paid for the copies and went home. When I arrived at home, I looked through the certificates, wondering who these couples were and if they were related to me.

I had heard family members mention various names when I was growing up, but I did not pay them much attention. I wanted to identify the names. I asked my aunts and uncles about the first names of my father's parents. I knew the last name of my grandfather's mother because of the constant reference of being related to those families while growing up. My grandfather's father's name was Augustus Bishop. An aunt had made copies of a picture of him to give to several members of the family at the same time I inquired. I also was reminded he worked for the Pennsylvania Railroad and lived in Camden, New Jersey. He supposedly died in Atlantic City. My grandfather's mother was named Celesta Durbin.

After talking with family, I looked in my folder of marriage certificates and located a paper with the names of my grandfather's parents. The copy included a very simple statement certifying they were united in marriage on December 14, 1898, at Havre de Grace, Maryland, signed by Reverend R. F. Green, pastor of AME Church. Finally, after hours of searching, I had found written, historical proof, a documentary link to the Bishop family for generations to come.

During the early years of my family search, not knowing or asking how to do research caused me to make many mistakes. I made many presumptions about the family name. I thought all families with the same surname were closely related, hence my collection of files on individuals with surnames, like the Bishop, Bond, and Harris families. Initially, I collected marriage, death, and census information without making any definite family connections or links to one another. I found myself in the courthouse blindly collecting names from the index books of marriage licenses, wills, and land records.

Realizing I was wasting time, energy, and money, and unable to connect most names with my family, I finally decided to get help. My new approach began with reading books on genealogy and attending workshops researching family history. I purchased genealogy software to keep track of my research, even though I had not much confirmed family to input. The how-to-start tutorials for beginners and various genealogy links were very helpful in encouraging my search of my family's roots.

As my search continued with browsing and making copies of the census records, my folders were getting rather bulky. I was putting in a whole lot of time and spending many quarters, but I was not making any headway with linking family members. I started to evaluate my family search process. I put the census copies in order and took note of the names and matched them with the marriage certificates I had collected. Since I viewed the older census schedules to start with, I noticed most of the Bishop family lived in the Emmorton area between 1850 and1880. Only one household family lived in Havre de Grace during this time. I took a closer look at this family, knowing that they lived in this town where my father and I had grown up.

Tracing family from the present back to the past, I located my grandfather's father and mother, along with his siblings, in the 1920 census schedules in Philadelphia. According to the census, there was but one Bishop family living in the town of Havre de Grace in 1910 and 1900. There are no records of the 1890 federal census due to a fire that destroyed a large portion of the documents. Even though I was unable to search Augustus Bishop further back in the census schedules, clues to who his family was still existed. I remembered the sole Bishop family discovered earlier in the 1860, 1870, and 1880 censuses in the town. So my research advanced to find out more of this family to answer the question of whether or not they were connected to my grandfather's father, Augustus Bishop.

I have learned in the process of tracing my family roots that research is about clues. There are documentary tracks to the past—vital information about us and our activities. What clues were there to the past in seeking facts about my grandfather's father, Augustus Bishop? I began to think of ways to track down and retrieve records of my ancestor. The census information is crucial in confirming family stories and in providing clues to other documents of information. What intrigued me about Augustus was his moving and working for the Pennsylvania Railroad. My imagination exploded with thoughts of expeditions through small towns and big cities along the East Coast. In my mind's eye, I pictured my tall, regal great-grandfather impressively dressed in a porter's uniform, greeting and serving guests for first-class rail travel. I wanted documentary details.

The best way to get personal history details about my great-grandfather Augustus Bishop was to start with the latest information on him. Relatives had given me sketchy stories to follow up on, and I was still searching for his obituary and death certificate. Upon writing letters requesting information, I got a response from the New Jersey vital records department indicating the need for exact dates in order to retrieve a death certificate. The Camden Historic Society's database only found him as a resident in the city directory with his second wife, Leila, in 1940, 1943, and 1947.

I turned to Social Security records. In 1935, the first Social Security card was issued, and applications were required to determine future benefits based on workers' earnings. I learned that railroad workers registered were issued special numbers up to July 1, 1963, and then they were given a number according to the state it was issued in. Following up on family talk, I wrote to the Railroad Retirement Board Office of Public Affairs, inquiring about genealogical information on great-grandfather Bishop. They informed me that there was a nonrefundable fee to locate any available records and to allow forty to sixty days for the search. Immediately, I sent a check with the fee, and fifteen days later, information on Pop Augustus was in my hand. They sent me a form CER-1, Social Security Carrier Employee Registration Application for Account Number, typed and signed February 2, 1937.

Augustus Bishop

807 Kaighn Ave., Camden, NJ
Employer: The Pennsylvania Railroad
Age: 62; Date of Birth: Nov. 29, 1874

Place of Birth: Havre de Grace, MD
Father: Isaac Bishop; Mother: Rachel Scott
Male X; Negro X
Date: 2-2-1937
Signed, Augustus Bishop

Written at the top of the index-sized copy of this original card was the nine-digit Social Security account number. The second page had a chart printed with a breakdown of service and earnings that were reported to the Interstate Commerce Commission from 1937-1946. For twelve months of work, the record revealed that in 1937 my great-grandfather earned $1,435.43 as a station attendant/bagman in the parcel room. Although very helpful, the report shattered my image of my great-grandfather's work career. In the last year, 1946, he worked eight months and reported earning $1,232.87. Even though my great-grandfather did not work as a first-class porter on a train, he did have a steady job as a station attendant in the baggage room. The information supplied by Pop Augustus on his SS application allowed me to continue my journey to fill details of my family's past.

The first known record on my grandfather's father was in the 1880 census schedule. He is listed as five-year-old grandson Gus in the household of Isaac Bishop with Rachel, located in the city of Havre de Grace, Maryland. During the 1880s, the city was growing in importance, carrying freight and passengers through the East Coast's major cities. The railroad had been constructed not only from the south through the small town but along the Susquehanna River into Lancaster, Pennsylvania, as well. The Tidewater Canal was equally important in transporting supplies up and down the Susquehanna River to and from large ships that made their way from the Atlantic Ocean into the Chesapeake Bay. A host of vessels, people, and commodities continued to go through this small city.

Pop Augustus Bishop was raised among the travelers, veterans, and industrious workers after the Civil War. I can imagine him looking out of his bedroom window just yards from the busy canal waterway and railroad stop along the river. The Havre de Grace community, like others throughout the country, was helping reconstruct the nation. Additionally, most African Americans were attempting to establish and redefine their identity. Many displaced people wandered into this small city, traveling through and looking for their place in life during this era of the lost instructive generation. Pop Augustus identified his grandparents as parents on his Social Security application of 1937. Whether or not he knew his biological parents is not yet certain. Evidently, my grandfather's father thrived among a close-knit community of family and friends. His elderly grandparents nurtured and instructed him in life's lessons as he and the community rapidly grew.

Just a few blocks from his home, Pop Augustus Bishop attended a school for black children called The Anderson Institute, on Linden Lane. In 1847, this property was purchased to build a church within the city. The challenge of raising enough money and in fighting among various opposing fractions hindered the building of a place of worship. On October 26, 1867 (WHD19 folio332), trustees agreed to purchase a part of this lot "for the purpose of a school for the colored people of the town of Havre de Grace…" Pop Augustus's intelligent former-slave grandfather was listed as a trustee, along with other African American men. The two-story Anderson Institute was built and named after a dedicated teacher, Mary Anderson.

Acquiring education was extremely difficult for African Americans in Harford County, Maryland. Segregation and attitudes of bigoted persons caused violence and bitter hostility to people of color. In one case, a teacher charged a white man with assault. She won her case; he received a slap on the wrist and was ordered to pay a petty fine. For speaking out, the teacher received a verbal lashing and became the subject of further humiliation and public ridicule.

Despite the many problems, it was a time of progress for the "People of Color" who transcended into African Americans after serving in the Civil War. These resilient people established institutions of value in their communities with the construction of churches, societies, and lodges. Many developed centers for learning and for people who, for centuries, were legally denied the privilege of reading and writing. A number of African Americans started businesses, purchased land, and sought out a higher education for their children.

My grandfather's father witnessed and experienced this progress during his lifetime. It seems the government underestimated the plight of reconstruction. Social programs were formed. Many schoolhouses were built, and a special bank was set up, all through an act creating the Freedmen's Bureau. Even with all this progress, the government became overwhelmed with the lack of money to support what it had created. The humanitarian need was much greater than many realized. Government programs to assist needy people and establish some sense of nationality failed and were shut down. Each African American community relied more heavily on itself and the churches, schools, and societies it had established.

Pop Augustus grew up in a supportive community despite racial differences. The school he attended was founded and supported by African Americans, even though it was supplemented by the government later. The church his family had attended was relocated within the town limits from outside the city's boundary line. Church history states that in the 1880s, the St. James AME Church building was physically moved by a team of horses from Chapel Road to its present location on Green Street.

On December 14, 1898, Augustus Bishop, age twenty-four years old, married Celesta A. Durbin, age eighteen years, in Havre de Grace. They are listed in Havre de Grace in the 1900 and 1910 federal census. In the land records, I discovered a 1915 court case between the St. James AME Church and the Baltimore & Ohio Railroad Company. The railroad needed a portion of land to rebuild a bridge across the Susquehanna River. This land was owned by the church and used as a united cemetery since the late 1800s. The court case lasted two years and resulted in condemning the property and moving the buried bodies to another nearby location, presently off Graceview Drive. These records listed my grandfather's father, Augustus Bishop, as trustee secretary of the St. James AME Church. Family members say he is buried in front of the united cemetery, along with trustee Samuel Ennis and with other Durbin, Brown, and Skinner family members.

Pop Augustus and other members are listed in a copy of the original minutes of the local Masonic lodge that they also established during this time. Even after moving to Philadelphia in 1917, he would travel back and forth to participate and support in its many ongoing community activities, demonstrating loyalty, honor, and dedication to the community of Havre de Grace.

Many African Americans leave little, if any, personal written records of their existence. Finding what remains is a gift. This is the frustrating challenge of researching family history. It becomes road blocks in the journey and often causes us to stop. Pop Augustus Bishop's involvement within the community had left a treasure trove of information to add depth to my family roots quest. On the other hand, the lack of recorded information on Mom Celesta has required far more investigating even deeper into the Durbin family.

Mom Celesta Durbin, according to the 1900 census, was born in April 1880. This was the only census schedule to include the month of a person birth, although many were inaccurate or omitted. Knowing the month of her birth helped me realized that she was born around the taking of the 1880 census. Most takers whose work occurred in the spring of the year did not record infants back then of less than a year. Meanwhile, I have researched Mom Celesta's relatives to make additional Durbin connections.

Stephen Durbin, married to Celesta Skinner, and his single sister, Jane Durbin, were the children of Bonaparte Durbin and Grace. As I look into the documents, Grace must had been enslaved or indentured to John Sappington, and Bonaparte was free. An 1832 Certificate of Freedom states:

Negro Bonaparte

Maryland, Harford County.

I hereby certify that the bearer hereof, Negro Bonaparte, twenty-five years of age, five feet, eight inches and a half high, dark complexion, rather slender-made, has a considerable lump just above the right knee, was born free and raised in Harford County.

In testimony whereof I have
hereby subscribed my name and
affixed the seal of Harford County
Court this thirteenth day of May, eighteen
hundred and thirty-two
Identified by Asaal Bailey
Henry Dorsey Clk.

Upon comparing names, ages, and information from the census schedules, I obtained copies of death certificates and Social Security applications to trace my Durbin family lineage. Nontraditional family settings challenge family history. Jane Durbin was listed as single with many children, natural born, and living near her brother, Stephen, who was married with two children. The death certificates added even more mystery. Jane's oldest son, Thomas, identified Martha Peaco—not Jane—as his mother. The father was listed as Isaac Durbin. I tried to decipher and match the information and came to this conclusion: the Durbin family was a family that took care of one another. Even though this is documented information, more research is pending to verify exact family connections.

Mom Celesta Durbin had close family living in Havre de Grace and on land along Chapel Road. Many of these were cousins who link unto present generations with family names like Brown, Dyson, Taylor, Hawkins, Ringgold, and Dorsey, to mention just a few.

Further in African American family history, linking a family unit may be all you have in tracing your roots. In my case, I focused on the unique names and geographic areas to make the association. The spelling within documents of the Durbin family was inconsistent at times. Variations in spelling are common: "Derbin," "Derban," "Durban," or even "Durrin." My Durbin family was consistent in retaining its name despite others incorrectly noting it. The family remains a part of Harford County history as it did back to earlier days when Durbins had owned taverns and operated the canal and extensions across the river with ferry boats since the 1700s.

I recall a story of relatives in Havre de Grace during the 1930s, then living in the canal lock house. Over the years, the keeper's house to the canal that paralleled the Susquehanna River had a variety of uses. At this time, my relatives had rented it with young children. Springtime floods and a heavy storm made the river rise so high that my Durbin relatives had to be rescued with a boat from the top floor of this historic house that today serves as a museum of local history.

My trails of information continue to grow, connecting links to amazing family history. Within the land records, I discovered one special 1815 record that added tremendously to my knowledge of the Bishop-Bond family's incredible past. It reads:

To Whom It May Concern, be it known that I, John Durbin, of Harford County in the state of Maryland, for divers good causes me thereunto moving, and in consideration of the natural love and affection I, the said John Durbin, have for my children herein after named have released, liberated, manumitted, and set free and by these do hereby release, liberate, manumit, and set free all my male children at the age of twenty-one years and my female children at the age of sixteen, their names and ages as follows:

Stephen Durbin, born the twenty-eighth day of March, seventeen hundred and ninety-one

Grace Durbin, born the twenty-ninth day of October, seventeen hundred and ninety-five

Hannah Durbin, born the fifth day of August, seventeen hundred and ninety-six

Harriet Durbin, born the twenty-ninth day of June, seventeen hundred and ninety-eight

Susan Durbin, born the tenth day of March, eighteen hundred

Mary Durbin, born the fourth day of January, eighteen hundred and two

Isabella Durbin, born the eighteenth day of January, eighteen hundred and four

Bonaparte Durbin, born the fourteenth day of September, eighteen hundred and five

Elizabeth Durbin, born the twenty-fifth day of June, eighteen hundred and eight

Christian Durbin, born the twenty-ninth day of August, eighteen hundred and ten

Bennett Durbin, born the twentieth day of December, eighteen hundred and thirteen

And then my said children named Stephen, Grace, Hannah, Harriet, Susan, Mary, Isabella, Bonaparte, Elizabeth, Christian, and Bennett. I do declare to be free and manumitted, that is to say the males from the time they have arrived or may arrive at the age of twenty-one years, and the females of sixteen years from the day of their birth as herein before written from all manner of servitude of service to me, my executors, or administrators forever. In the testimony whereof, I have hereunto set my hand and affixed my seal this 28th day of March in the year of our Lord, eighteen hundred and fifteen.

His sign sealed and delivered in the presence of
JohnXDurbin
Thomas Jeffery
William Bowen

Harford County to wit on this 28th day of March 1815 personally appear John Durbin party to the within instrument of writing before me subscriber a justice of the peace of the state of Maryland for the said county and acknowledge the same to be his act and deed for the purpose within mentioned and the several children therein named to be discharged.

John Durbin had legally liberated all his children during this crucial time in America's history, recorded in land record

HDG Y 266. I could not help but be overjoyed to have been able to connect links of my family. My grandfather had said, "You kids are related to all of Harford County." I had traced most of the links to these eleven children, and the family names link most of the county with families like Wilson, Presbury, Hopkins, Giles, Wesley, Young, and Kennard. Kennard is a direct family line to my mom on her mother's side.

John Durbin purchased more than fifty acres of land over many years, starting in 1811. Court records reveal many transactions under John Gilbert Durbin. I can surmise that as a free man of color, using various middle names or even a third added more credibility to a person's status. Most blacks were addressed by one name, and the whites had three or more. Pop John, "Jack," used John D. Gilbert and John G. Durbin in court documentations. I noticed that he signed with an "X." Was it a screen, for many laws at that time did not allow blacks to be able to read nor write? I can just imagine white Quaker or abolitionist friends helping along the legal process, preparing documents and serving as witnesses. Pop John Gilbert Durbin purchased land, freed his children, completed work orders, and left a will for me to discover in the trial of time, tracing my family history. In 1836, Bonaparte was the administrator of the said will, which included all the *married* names of the daughters Pop John "Jack" Gilbert Durbin had freed in 1815.

SOMEHOW
I MADE IT

My youth was a sheer delight, with inner strength and great vitality despite diabetes. On the other hand, looking back over my young adult years, it amazes me how I made it. It was God who kept sustaining me and putting protective angels around me and instilling within my being His Spirit of guided peace. While working full time in the accounting office, I attended Bible college and seminary full time. I still volunteered when I was not doing ministry within the church activities and service. I wonder how I did this continually for more than two years straight. It did not seem so bad doing something I enjoyed, especially God's ministry with children and singing. These passions motivated me to press on, even when physically exhausted.

I believe that same passion for God's service and people was embedded within my family and was a major part of my upbringing. I remember traveling with the youth choir, directed by my aunt and cousin, to nursing homes and convalescent centers to sing to its residents who were in wheelchairs and hospital beds. This small act left a lasting impression on me and the many other youths in this group. In the early 1970s, a youth choir for the church had been formed, called "The Young Generation," from all the neighborhood young people around the Gravel Hill church. We would travel, sing at various churches and accompany the pastor. I remember practicing every Saturday afternoon at 1:00 p.m. Before the group was formed, the community organized its own park and recreation program to keep the many young people busy playing sports and games. Around the holidays, various groups took time to visit one another's homes, singing carols and gospel songs. With or without music accompaniment, Gravel Hill groups could sing. They often sang as if angels joined in with them. I strongly believe ancestors within our community joined in certain songs, which seemed to take off in an extremely spiritual way.

In 1982, St. James AME Church in Gravel Hill was supplied and then appointed its first woman pastor. Reverend Violet H. (Garnett) Tann was instrumental in the dramatic growth in outreach ministry and directed an extensive renovation of the church by its own members. The men of the church and community, including my uncles, worked night and day on this major undertaking. I can remember placing a couple of floor tiles and cleaning when I was not working or going to college. Many families joined and attended the church, and we traveled to various places with Reverend Tann as a unified church family.

I have been blessed to endure economic hardship despite my being better off than many. For many years, financial situations kept me against the wall; most of the time, it had been of my own careless misdoings. I lived paycheck to paycheck when it did not have to be. It had been normal for me to spend all I had on others, the church, and family, not thinking about my own needs. My father's mismanagement of finances set a very poor example for me. Now I often think of my great-uncle who said, "We are in for a hard winter, but we'll get through it." "Stay encouraged" is the lesson I have learned and realize in my lifetime.

As children, we were not exposed to the idea of financial management as being a means to securing the future. My concept of management was generations of working hard for very little and surviving on a day-after-day basis. African Americans were introduced to the banking system only after the Civil War, in which a select few were able to participate. The plight of just getting by and no need to worry of tomorrow entrenched a "spend what you got now" attitude instead of having monetary investments work for you. I could organize my money to spend, but I failed to control it to invest. Most African Americans have just been passive products of capitalism, not active participants with a secure plan for the future. I thank God that I have avoided the necessity of being involved in harmful acts for the sake of survival.

While living in Baltimore City, I had observed street lessons in survival. I criticized no one for doing what they needed to do to sustain themselves. Most of the ugly acts I saw were because of an unshakable habit of unhealthy addictions that plunged some people into an overwhelming sense of desperation. The vile development of slavery in America was absolutely despicable, and the addictive drug cultures in its many complex forms are themselves a form of slavery.

When I first started living in Baltimore, I had to adjust to the city. I would speak to everyone who spoke, naïve as I may have been. I often thought the people to be horribly rude in the way they aggressively asked for what they wanted, with no shame or humility. "Hey, brother, can you spare a dollar?" If you reached to get a dollar, they would ask for five or ten. Hustle was, for some, the game and lifestyle of urban living to survive.

Attending workshops and meetings on business opportunities was one of my major activities when I first moved to the city. Some may have been scams or get-rich-quick schemes that never amounted to much after receiving an initial setup or paying a starter-kit fee. City life just amplified the hustle of people doing what they could to get the money they wanted. I suppose the reason I did not have much money was because I seemed not to care once the money was gone, even though I wished I had more to do charitable things with. I have been overly generous for my own good. I have given away my coats, watches, Bibles, and the last dollars in my pocket when I sensed someone genuinely was in need. Some of the homeless people had joined me as I treated them to a submarine sandwich. Every so often, I wished the favor had been an instant return in my times of need, but God gave me patience to endure until my needs had been met.

Many times I noticed cunning ways some people employed to survive, and I soon realized a subtle urban language that existed within city culture. For instance, one night I was parking my car a block away from my aunt's house, and a woman approached as I was gathering my lunch bag and items. She waved five dollars toward me and said, "Take me somewhere."

Before I knew it, she had opened the car door and sat in the passenger seat, as if I agreed to drive her to where she needed to go. Her mouth was going without stopping. "I will take care of you. I'll do this and that."

As nice as I tried to be to this woman, she would not get out of my car. With the sternest voice I could mimic, I angrily said, "Get your &@*# out my car." She finally got out, fussing and cussing, sashaying her way down the sidewalk. It was as if the only way she understood was with ruthless, foul language.

I suppose it does not always pay to be nice. Many of us live in an emotionally isolated or imbalanced world, especially cultivated within the close confines of city living. But a sense of cold-heartedness and an attitude of "So what?" about everything could consume your being. Sometimes I found myself speaking loudly and somewhat rudely, infected by urban culture. Even though the enticing allure of big city hustles and culture was strong, my deep-rooted sensibility and upbringing enabled me to reject its seductions. I believe the great stability of my Bishop-Bond family's identity of who I am helped me endure morally in a correct manner. I am stubbornly set in my small-town ways. Life has tested my strength, faith, and stability. God and my family values have allowed me to persevere.

I hold on to things. After years of driving a car like *The Flintstones* and seeing the road through the floor, my father and I shopped for and purchased a newer car on a Saturday afternoon. That night I drove the car and parked in front of my aunt's house, only to have a motorcycle smash into it. The mirror was totally crushed. Paint had been scraped off, and a huge dent was on the driver's side. The motorcycle rider kept on going. I could not file a claim through insurance because it had not been transferred yet. The dealer had let me test drive it home, even though I had decided to buy it, and was waiting for the next business day to complete the purchase. Fortunately, my talented uncles repaired the damage, and I was satisfied with my car for more than ten years.

I worked two jobs full time for more than four years while living in the city. After working in the accounting office during the day, at night I worked in an Italian pizza carryout. It was nice that I could become family to many people. The Italian owners took me on a private jet to a new casino boat in Mississippi; we had such a good time. This job lasted until the owner moved and sold the store several years later.

Also in Baltimore, I worked in an accounting office and volunteered for Health Education Resource Organization, mentoring patients living with AIDS. The "Buddy Program" matched me up with patients who could interact and talk with me. I helped with various nonprofit fundraising activities to help the organization throughout the Baltimore area. My major time was just being there with my "buddy."

My buddy's name was Grady; he and I were two of a kind. We liked many of the same things, and our personalities were similar. The organization knew exactly what they were doing when it came to matching. I helped Grady move to his own place, and if he needed to talk, I would be there. He had a walking stick for stability to support his very thin, five feet ten inch frame. I was working and traveling home to Harford County every weekend. Naturally, I talked about my family, and he wanted to meet them, as they wanted to meet him. We went to church in Harford County and dinner at Aunt Dot's, the aunt I lived with in the city. Grady enjoyed the time with my church family who sang his favorite song, "His Eye Is on the Sparrow."

As I reflect over the challenges that I have had to confront, I cannot imagine what my ancestors had gone through. Somehow I made it, and I would not be here if they had not overcome. My journey of discovery of my family roots reawakens my realization of self. At times it's as if I lived it with my ancestors. Of course, the scope of their challenges far exceeded those I experienced. God is how I made it; God is how they made it.

Turn of the Twentieth Century

It started in the year 1900, an era of great change as veterans and a lost generation ushered in a new century of traditionalists. At the turn of the century, a majority of the citizens in the United States lived in towns having a population of less than 2,500. The United States of America was more rural than urban but was already a world leader in industry. The United States was benefiting from both a great abundance in natural resources and an economy organized by giant corporations. The United States led the world in the production of iron and steel, promoted by the rise of factories like the Bethlehem Steel Plant in Sparrows Point, Maryland. The United States also produced much of the world's cotton, corn, and oil and a third of its coal and gold. The United States was also experiencing growth in agriculture, with self-sufficient, diversified farms giving way to specialized commercial agriculture.

In rural areas, many people were poor. In inner cities, overworked factory workers lived in crowded and unsanitary tenements. Yet, in general, at the beginning of the century, people in the United States could buy more than they had in previous decades. More farm products were abundantly available in the cities, and therefore, these products were cheaper. With the rise of industry had come an increase in the variety and abundance of goods. Traffic increased via railroad, ships, and cargo carts, especially over mainstream routes through towns like Havre de Grace, Maryland. The automobile, or "horseless carriage," was just beginning to make its appearance in the United States, disturbing the city traffic of horse-drawn wagons and bicycles. Electricity was reaching more people in cities, propelling new electric trolley cars that increased people's mobility. A Brooklyn baseball team acquired the name "Dodgers" from the ability of its fans to dodge trolley cars.

At the turn of the century, it had been only thirty-five years since the American Civil War had ended, and Negroes, as they were then called, had not yet acquired equality. The victorious North had only briefly disenfranchised the South's white leaders, who soon returned to lead a reactionary movement. The failure of Reconstruction, for the most part, left African Americans without property, wealth, and education. At the turn of the century, many blacks in the South were still working on plantations or as tenant farmers and sharecroppers. In Harford County, many rented tenant homes near farms and worked as laborers on them, in contrast to the relative prosperity of other disadvantaged ethnic groups.

In 1896, the Supreme Court, in a case called *Plessy v. Ferguson*, sided with Southern segregationist states that wanted "separate but equal" facilities for blacks. In addition, by the turn of the century, many Southern whites were exercising what discrimination they could with the Jim Crow laws. "Whites Only" and "Colored Only" signs appeared, as did laws describing where blacks could and could not reside, attend church, eat, use public toilets, or drink water. Laws appeared, prohibiting the ultimate in integration between the races: intermarriage. And outside the South, most whites either cared little about segregation in the South or they welcomed it. Throughout America, these same sentiments of white racial superiority predominated. Harford County promoted segregation through the Board of School Commissions, the political establishment, the business community, and other institutions of life.

At the turn of the century, vigilantism still existed. Lynching was its common method. Most of the lynching of whites, by whites, took place in the western states. In the South—Maryland included—it was whites who were lynching blacks, although the lynching of blacks also occasionally took place outside the South, where blacks were fewer in number. In 1900, many African American males were lynched. Many indeed had committed a rape, but others were wrongfully accused. On the other hand, if a white man raped an African American woman, he might be fined only twenty dollars.

Few jobs existed in the South and West for largely unskilled black workers. Filled with hope for a better life, many blacks migrated north, only to discover employers were hiring immigrant whites. Blacks in the North also found urban slums prejudiced. For those jobs black workers did secure, they often received half the pay white laborers were given. Stereotypical songs and shows made a bad situation worse.

ENDURANCE
WITHIN
COMMUNITY

On January 14, 1966, I was about one and a half years old. My grandmother, Sarah Amelia Bond-Bishop, died from complications of diabetes and high blood pressure. Her father, George, named her after his mother, Sarah. Family and friends say she was just as beautiful within as in her lovely outer appearance. Genuine and unique, her gentleness, kindness, and hospitality were toward all she would meet. When it comes to my character traits and personality, it seems I am compared to my grandmother's side of the family. Often when growing up, from out of nowhere, my aunt or uncle would call me "Pop Bond." I suppose the way I carried myself and the mannerisms reminded them of their father, grandfather, and my great-grandfather, George W. Bond.

My father's mother's father, my great-grandfather, died July 9, 1944, from heart problems. The death certificate states his full name as George Washington Bond, born on March 5, 1873, in Pennsylvania to Harry Bond and Sarah. There is an apparent discrepancy in the records in regards to his birth year. The census schedules list the year of his birth as 1867. I found discrepancies like this not uncommon in researching African American genealogy possibly for reasons of illiteracy or lack of interest in accuracy on behalf of the census taker, or just translator error.

Like Pop Augustus Bishop, during "Pop George Bond's" lifetime, many changes occurred within the society around him. Those born during Reconstruction like Pop Bond learned that adaptability and resourcefulness were major keys to survival. My father's mother's father's death certificate and census records state he was born in Pennsylvania. Family members say, more specifically, it was in an area called Peach Bottom. For whatever reason, his parents moved to Hopewell, Maryland, while he was very young. The earliest record found was with his parents and siblings in the 1880 census. He is listed as George W., age fifteen, in the household of Henry Bond and Sarah, with four brothers and one sister. The 1890 census was destroyed by fire, which adds to the challenge of family history research.

My great-grandfather George Bond was a pioneer in moving his family and pursuing a job with the soon-to-be VA hospital. He was like my Pop Augustus Bishop, moving an entire family to a big city to work for the railroad as a luggage baggage man. Both of the Bishop and Bond fathers had a clear vision of what to do for the advancement of family while actively making contributions to the overall community.

I found that researching before the turn of the twentieth century for African American families becomes challenging. There are very few records that exist. Many persons have no other documented information except for the census records, and some even lack them. Recordkeeping of family events like births, marriages, and deaths was a perplexing mental reality, in that many blacks after the Civil War had only recently learned to read and write. The community, reprised by laws against reading and writing for African Americans, infused a cognitive reluctance and inadequate ability to prioritize the importance of written documentation.

If any records ever existed, mismanagement of records often led to their loss, especially church records. Many black institutions relied on a few individuals to safeguard records by taking them home, with little accountability. Once those individuals were no longer active, the records got lost and forgotten by the organization. Many records have been completely damaged, destroyed, and neglected by people who did not know their importance nor had any idea of their direct relevance for future generations.

Pop George Bond remained close with his siblings from Pennsylvania after the Civil War and moved to Hopewell around the early 1870s. The brothers and sisters moved near each other as they came back to the area of their father's birth. Several relatives and distant cousins remain in touch even today. This connection, evident at family gatherings, has helped lead to links confirming kinships before vital records existed in my research.

Newspapers, unlike private records, often remain to yield valuable family information. I was delighted to have come across the following two articles:

Southern Aegis Newspaper
March 6, 1891

"Little Locals from Level"
Reported for the *Aegis*

Feb.25 – Harry Bond, an aged colored man living near here, died last Saturday morning, Feb 21st, and was buried at Greenspring Cemetery on the following Tuesday afternoon. He was eighty-six yrs of age and resided in this vicinity for the past fifteen years. During that time his conduct was exemplary, and he enjoyed the confidence and esteem of his neighbors.

Harford Democrat
March 6, 1891

Wm. H. Bond, colored, aged eighty-five years, eleven months, and twenty-one days, died at his son's home near Level, Saturday last. He leaves a wife, six sons, three daughters, and twelve grand-children. He was buried on Monday at Green Spring Chapel, of which he was a member for over fifty years. Rev. P.H. Green of Havre de Grace conducted the service. J.B. Bailey, undertaker.

These two articles gave me specific information and confirmed family stories of living in Level (Hopewell) and attending Greenspring Church. This article was an obituary about my father's mother's father's father, William H. Bond, Pop George Bond's father. With this find in the newspaper article, I could confirm the name, number of children, and calculate the day he was born. In my search, I had come across many names with popular and variations, like William H. Bond. Even though his family had moved here fifteen years ago from Pennsylvania, he attended this church for more than fifty years. My conclusion is that he was born and raised near this area where he died and was buried. His son George was twenty-four, with his wife, Amelia, and a baby daughter when the funeral service occurred.

The census records list several more children over the decades within the Bond household; it's not certain whether they were all children of Henry and Sarah. In those days children would be raised by other relatives, especially when the family had grown rather large. I list them in tribute, especially to my cousins who remain closely connected, sharing family times.

Edward Bond married Susan Lee and had two sons.

Catherine Bond married George Rumsey, had son Harry Rumsey

Sarah E. Bond married George Brisco, four children

William H. Bond married Martha Adams, had eleven children

Joshua Bond married Josephine Prigg, had seven sons

John W. Bond married Mary Webster

Martha J. Bond married first a Howard and second a William Thompson, with a total of seven children

Hezekiah Bond married Julia Kenly

James A. Bond

Pop George Washington Bond married Amelia Harris, had eight children

Frank L. Bond

Mary Sophia Bond married John W. Johnson

David T. Bond married Mary Baty, had eight children

These were the children of Pop Harry Bond and Sarah A. E. Prigg, who lived in Peach Bottom during the Civil War and returned home to Harford County, Maryland. There are many links of my family who make up who I am; these are just a small part of the many other Bond family members. On August 18, 1889, Pop George W. Bond married Amelia A. Harris, at St. James AME, Gravel Hill. This Bond family link to the Harris family continues my link generations back. Mom Amelia grew up on Gravel Hill in the "home place" house owned by her father's second wife, Mary Dorsey, cousin and adopted daughter on the Bishop-Durbin family line.

Pop George Bond's wife, Mom Amelia, was born on November 28, 1872, to Lawson and Margaret Harris, the eighth of nine children born to this union. Most of her life, she worked with her husband and family as a domestic. In 1933, Amelia and George moved from Perrypoint to the area she always had known as a child. They purchased land close to the Gravel Hill church property previously owned by the Stokes family. I believe they had intended on moving back to this area early from Perrypoint VA Hospital but allowed their daughter and her family to settle first. The deed of the home place where my grandparents resided was purchased by Pop George and Mom Amelia years before. I know that there was a strong bond of this community and the Bond family.

My aunts were practically raised by their grandparents, Pop George and Mom Amelia. The home place was only a few hundred yards down the road. Family lived all around the area, taking care of one another. The couple stimulated modern growth and updates with the drilling of water wells, subdividing of lots with new dwellings, and the installation of electricity throughout the modest community. A public road lined with poles and wires opened this once rather isolated safe haven for free people of color to the rest of the community.

As kids, we walked, played, and rode our bikes on the road countless times. With only two or three dim lights on poles along the road, the darkness of the night was illuminated by the brilliant stars. I remember lying on the grassy bank and looking to the sky. From my view, the sky seemed crystal clear and gleamed with each noticeable constellation. I would get excited and make a wish as streaks of a shooting star every now and then would appear. This experience so piqued my interest to question my father about the Big and Little Dipper, as well as the obviously bright North Star. This one star shined so intensely that I felt I could reach out and touch it. At the time, I did not realize that along this path in the quiet, clear, still of the night, this exact same star had guided so many runaways and enslaved people of color through this area north to freedom.

I think of independence, support, security, and freedom when recalling my growing up in Gravel Hill. The peace, tranquility, and stability were always a constant draw and sanctuary for me. Living in Baltimore City with my aunt, I hardly ever failed to return home on the weekends. I contemplated staying in the city and contributing to its local church ministry. But there was just something about attending my home church in Gravel Hill, that I did not mind the travel every week. My routine was to work during the day Monday through Friday and drive to choir rehearsal on the first Monday nights. My cleaning company had me working from time to time in Harford County twice a week. The full schedule often had me working all night. I wonder how I physically did it, especially adding full-time college and another job to my already-crammed scheduled.

My aunt in Baltimore was wonderful, very concerned, and caring but not intrusive about what I was doing. Living with her gave me a sense of stable support and independence that I needed. I am eternally grateful for Aunt Dottie's spirit of optimistic encouragement, caring, and togetherness. As a child, my brother, sister, and I looked forward to her visits on weekends. We considered her the "soul lady" from the city who would update us on the latest trends and popular gadgets. I often wondered how she could get so much stuff in bags she had traveled with on the bus. It was always a treat to see what she had in her bag. She made jewelry and other items that we often sold. I enjoyed packing my mom's car and driving along the road to find a nice busy spot to set up tables and signs to sell what we had: dog-tag chains, flower globes, household goods, and other jewelry and yard-sale items.

My aunt would always have a treat of information or a new idea of doing things for funds or fun. I had the time of my life going on a bus trip to Wild Wood, New Jersey, with her friends. She would take periodic groups on excursions called a mystery tour, and she would end up somewhere, having a dancing good time after a crab feast in a place we had never visited before. Not only were these events enjoyable, but they nurtured a whole new perspective on things and life in general. My aunt Dot took the Bishop-Bond attributes to another exciting level that continues to excite me.

According to family members, Mom Amelia Bond was a very quiet, supportive wife to her husband George and family. They would turn the old schoolhouse into an ice cream parlor as a treat to the community. She would make homemade ice cream and treats that everyone highly anticipated. I can imagine neighborhood kids finding out through talk that Mom Bond was churning homemade treats to be served at the schoolhouse. She was the youngest daughter of nine born to Lawson and Margaret Harris. Her siblings were:

Laura V. Harris married Jarret H. Stokes, had five children

Malachi Harris, minister, married Annie Chambers, 2nd M. Peaco

John Harris, born about 1860

Lawson Harris T.G. married Susanna Brown, had seven children (daughter Ida was the caterer in Philadelphia)

Zanica A Harris married Stephen Preston

Caleb Harris, born 1864

Jacob Harris, born 1866

Mom Amelia A. Harris married George Bond, had eight children

Lewis Francis Harris, born 1873

The Reconstruction Period

Between 1867 and 1877, a total rebuilding of the United States and its communities occurred throughout much of the country. Mom Amelia and her family had liberty within the confines of the close-knit community, but the country as a whole had gone through a transformation. Even though Maryland had been a border state between the free and enslaved, people of color had to wrestle with the reality of those refusing to accept the change. Suppression, distinct cultural differences, and the ingrained way of doing things were difficult to integrate. The nation had to repair itself physically, mentally, and spiritually. For many years, free African Americans had helped advance the plight of those enslaved; most of them were possibly family members. Now both family members and the race of people needed much help and assistance. Many missionary and humanitarian organizations provided necessary services. Many new churches were established and were fully active, along with societies and fraternities.

Well established within society, the Bishop and Bond families were very instrumental in establishing communal organizations, like schools, churches, and fraternal groups. The Good Samaritans group was very active in alleviating various social issues, even to the point of paying local funeral directors for burial of those who were unable to afford it.

Many societies provided shelter, food, and the basic necessities. People of color struggled to establish themselves as viable American citizens. Because they were ostracized and often shunned for their color, their opportunities toward progress to better their livelihood were limited. Those African Americans who were established with land and sustenance were bound to aid the plight of others needing help and education and knew how to plan their means of living. This communal sense, whether out of best moral obligation or pure conscience, borne by association because of the color in the skin obligated a connection to improve conditions for the advancement of their race of people. The government's effort to provide programs was underestimated by the overall need of a split nation. Programs initially started to help with African American finances and education were overwhelmed and collapsed under their own support.

The Freedmen's Bureau helped many refugees with food, housing, and health issues. It oversaw a formal system of education for African Americans in the South. The Bureau operated from 1865 to 1871. It was disbanded because of several financial burdens and threats that it helped promote an organization against former slaveholders. Organizations, especially the churches, moved to fill the void to continue the services to their own community. African American education continued years later in the Anderson and McComas Institutes, Hosanna School, and other local schools in the Harford County area.

The Bishop-Bond family was actively involved in the support of its community. Mom Amelia's parents purchased land at Gravel Hill to give their family a stable life. Her father, Lawson, a former slave, and Margaret Hill, born to free parents, raised a family through the toughest of times within a close and supportive family.

I am who I am as links of my family. They influenced who I am by the environment I was raised in and the things I have been exposed to. Growing up in a small community, our immediate family often went away to an amusement park or beach during the summer months. But these experiences were nothing compared to visits from out-of-town family members. I would learn more from my uncles and aunts than any other source of learning. My father's sister Aunt Dot often visited and cooked for the family. I learned about and how to prepare soul food. She always had something new in a bag. I often found myself asking what that was. Unlike my father, I would try anything at least once. I recall ox tails, hog maws, spoon bread, pig tails with beans, and chitterlings. My aunt Dot introduced me to all types of garden greens, like collards, kale, mustard, and turnip leaves. I watched and listened as she instructed us on how to clean and cut the stems. The traditional key to great taste is adding the smoked ham hock and then letting it cook tenderly slow to soak in flavor. I stopped being surprised to wake up in the mornings to the aroma of something cooking and smelling very good. I often could not get enough of a favorite breakfast, butterfish and beans.

CIVIL WAR IN AMERICA

Other than the crude woman in my car in Baltimore, I can hardly think of an instance in which I've had a heated exchange or argument with anyone. I had some misunderstandings, but they were nothing of any great consequence. I do recall, however, one dramatic episode in my youth that now, looking back, was much of a prompted exhibition.

The number of neighborhood kids increased as I entered middle-school age. We still had a close group, with younger siblings following after us as we went about hanging out and playing. We only had minor scuffles, but nothing too major, as we still looked out for one another. Middle school brought about a totally new dynamic, as kids from several elementary schools around the area came together.

I made many new friends, but the vast number of young people created a highly agitated rumor mill. I was a quiet person who did not talk to too many people, usually only close friends. I would talk to those I had classes with, knew at church, or lived close to in our neighborhood. For the most part, I got along with all, except this one guy who would eye me from a distance in the cafeteria or in the hall. I tried to avoid him because he was loud and taunted others for no reason. He and I did not see eye-to-eye. From a distance, he would intently stare at me with intimidating looks. I suppose he tried to get a reaction or response from me and my friends, which he never did at school.

All during school, neighborhood friends constantly told me things this guy said about me. I had not said nor done anything to him. I heard he wanted to beat me up. My brother was mouthy and scrappy, often joining in on the talk, day and night, escalating the rumors throughout the neighborhood. Words did not bother me as much as they did my brother. I was the cool, calm, collected person in intense situations, whereas he would explode, ranting and raving as if vague threats would solve or calm a situation.

School had closed for the summer vacation, and kids primarily stayed within their designated neighborhoods. My neighborhood was located between two highways near a huge cemetery. Our homes were lined on a road that looped through our community, called "the Manor." We knew who was who, and kids hardly ventured to or from our neighborhood or others. Besides the skateboarding, ball games, marbles, and just hanging out, this summer was a little different.

As fate would have it, the guy who taunted and talked of beating me up had to stay the summer with his grandmother. She lived in my neighborhood around the corner and on the way to the 7-Eleven store from my house. The neighborhood kids talked, and the rumor mill churned intensely as it seemed to throughout the whole town. A friend and I routinely walked to the store, always to get a treat. We strolled this time with confrontational curiosity to see if it was true that he lived here. We knocked on his grandmother's door and asked about him. She said she had not seen him all day; he was riding his bike and needed to come home. I was not sure what I would have done if I saw him at that time anyway.

In the meantime, my older cousin from Chester, Pennsylvania, came to visit and happened to be watching us younger kids for a day. The rumor mill had been brewing intensely for days, with little sight of this guy on my part, but friends saw him. My cousin was an instigator and stepped into an already extremely intense neighborhood situation.

I was in my house, content, and heard a gathering of chattering and sudden commotion outside. When I stepped to the door and looked out, I was surprised. It looked like more than a hundred kids had congregated in front of our house. I had never seen so many kids in our neighborhood before. They had come from all over town on foot, bikes, and skateboards. In the midst was a guy half hanging off his bike and being dragged to confront me in my front yard. This guy who intimidated and talked so much was whimpering and crying. My cousin pushed me out the door, and all I could hear was the crowd taunting and chanting, "What you gonna do now, mouthy, you big cry baby?"

It took me a few seconds to realize what was going on. I do not remember what happened next, but the guy and I were on the ground brawling. Kids were pushing us, yelling and screaming all around the muddy stream in back of my house. This guy and I both were crying, clutched together and rolling on the ground. That was it. Once I got up, I ran in the house and got the biggest knife I could find. Like a madman, I started chasing whoever was in my yard out and away. All kids scattered and started running, clearing out from around my house in a hurry. My cousin grabbed me and the knife. He was laughing, and I did not think any of it was funny. But these were no arguments or mishaps. After the confrontation, I could not believe how friendly this guy was every time we saw one another in the neighborhood and even later in school.

During the 1850s, arguments arose within the country on differing political issues, splitting the country into Northern states and Southern states. Unlike my childhood confrontation, history states that cousins fought against cousins. As time passed, the rights of the states often collided with actions the federal government was taking. Arguments arose over taxation, tariffs, internal improvements, the military, and, of course, slavery. It came to a boil when Lincoln became president, and the Southern states seceded. The resulting horrible Civil War concluded with a bitter unity.

Men of color, free and enslaved, were eager to enlist in the Union army. They were anxious to join the fight against slavery, and they believed that military service would allow them to prove their right to equality. Even the North was reluctant at first for black men to bear arms. Marylander Frederick Douglass was a strong advocate of allowing blacks to fight, believing this would prove their right to citizenship and the vote. He was an abolitionist who strongly believed that black soldiers were capable and willing to fight for their freedom if given the chance. One of the justifications for slavery in the minds of many Southerners was the supposed inferiority of blacks to whites; some claimed that blacks were like children who needed someone to care for them.

Men of color were allowed enrollment in 1862, and the Emancipation Proclamation permitted black men to enlist in the active military in January 1863. During the war, between 1862 and 1865, many stepped up to serve, as history records many of Harford County's heroic men of color even walked to Philadelphia, Pennsylvania, to join the Union army. Over 200 from Harford County alone fought for their freedom and of the colored race. Many enslaved persons were manumitted, freed to fight.

Eighteen Civil War black soldiers were given the Medal of Honor for their heroic service. Sadly, while voting rights and other equal rights were added to the Constitution, the Southern states found a way to get around these laws and continued to deprive blacks of many of the basic rights of the citizenship they had fought so hard to achieve.

Alfred B. Hilton, born about 1842, was age eight in the 1850 census and age twenty-three in 1860. He was the son of Isaac and Harriet Hilton, of Hopewell Cross Roads, and served as a sergeant in Co. H, 4th US Colored Troops, from August 11, 1863, until his death on October 21, 1864, at Hampton Hospital in Fort Monroe, Virginia. For his gallantry in action, he was awarded after death the Medal of Honor on April 8, 1865. He was a distant cousin of the Bond family.

In 1890, a census schedule for veterans of the Civil War pension eligibility was taken. I compared post offices and matched the areas on a map to get a general idea of where most former soldiers resided in the county. This is how I found my mother's mother's grandfather John Kennard in Churchville. He was listed, but because of his name's misspelling, after requesting other pension files, I received his records under John T. Kennett (Kennard). A letter within the file was from soldiers in the Hopewell area, where he had grown up, verifying his identity and eligibility, even though his last name was misspelled, to collect a pension. In tracing his ancestors, I found he also was a link to the Bishop side of the family as the son of Isabella Durbin, daughter of John Gilbert Durbin.

The Civil War was a monumental event in the lives of people of color across the nation and within the county of Harford in Maryland. Free people and former slaves had increased in numbers and had become firmly established within thriving communities. Colored troops returned home with new ideas, visions, and new perspectives. Many established and became involved in societies, lodges, schools, and churches. Before the war, opinions were strong for and against slavery. Harford County was part of a border state in which free people of color and slave owners existed side by side. Many took a vocal stand to demonstrate for their cause, especially Southern sympathizers, strongly for slavery.

Articles printed in *The Southern Aegis*
March 27, 1858
"Runaway Negroes"

Our town was thrown into a considerable excitement on Monday morning last, by the intelligence that a batch of Negroes had decamped from their owners and was on their way to Pennsylvania. As far as heard from, there were six in the party—three men belonging to Robert W. Holland, Esq., one man to Mrs. Lee, and a woman and child belonging to Henry W. Archer, Esq.

It appears that on Sunday afternoon about four o'clock, one of the Negroes hired a wagon of one of our citizens, to which was attached one of Mr.

Holland's mules, apparently for a little ride, since which time nothing has been heard of them.

Early Monday morning, a posse of the town, headed by Sheriff Whiteford, pursued in the direction of the Pennsylvania line, near which they found the mule and wagon in a fence corner. It is supposed from the rapid appearance of the river and heavy wind which prevailed on Sunday night that the party failed in crossing; hence there is a reasonable prospect of some of them at least being apprehended. Mr. Holland immediately offered a reward of $1000.00 dollars for the arrest of his boys, who are very valuable to him and who had been indulged to such an extent as to preclude all suspicion of any attempt or disposition to leave. There is no doubt the party had accomplices in their schemes, and a sharp look should be kept by our people to discover the lurking places of these "wolves in sheep's clothing," that they may receive a merited punishment.

This is another warning too to our officers of justice to see that all the laws relating to Negroes are strictly carried out, particularly those relating to their meeting together in secret societies—one of which we understand exist in our village at this very time.

A Break in the Action

Time takes no breaks with life as history continues to be made. Occasionally, my search for my family's roots became so intensive that I would need to take a brief break from my education in the practice of genealogy. As I review my several years' journey into my family history, the research takes a strategic turn in acquiring documentation before the arrival of the twentieth century.

The Reconstruction Period was a time of regrouping and finding a connection within the African American community. A whole culture and race of people had to adapt to another situation that involved their livelihood and liberty. A system of enslavement had compromised who they were, and this period of time was the start of defining who the people of color were within a society: African Americans.

In tracing my family roots from the current into the past, I am reminded of the trails in time we leave and that we share a common history with present generations, like my niece, nephews, and younger cousins. I reinforce my link through my generation in my sister and connect with a half brother as we memorialize a brother. I honor my roots in the support of my mother as we remember the life of my father and both their siblings. I connect through my vague memories my grandfather, Pop Oscar; his Philadelphian siblings; and my high regard to his wife, my grandmother Sarah, and her Bond siblings for their dedication to family and love for the church. My search proceeds to layer ancestral generations with Pop Augustus and his wife, Mom Celesta Durbin Bishop, who moved to Philly for a better economic life. Likewise, Pop George Bond, and his wife, Mom Amelia Harris Bond, were forerunners who helped advance Perrypoint Hospital and the community of Gravel Hill with electricity and social support.

My family research continues as I uncover a treasure trove of history in the Bishop-Bond connections during and before the Civil War. A county of cousins becomes evident through the Durbin family in that my mother's mother was a direct descendant within the family line. The home place had been a refuge for many generations in that Pop Lawson Harris with his wife, Margaret Hill-Harris, raised their family during the American Civil War. My family journey in linking tracks in time led to carpenter Pop Isaac Bishop, who purchased his wife, Mom Rachel Scott Bishop, from slavery, and built courteous integrity within the small city of Havre de Grace. This ancestral generation brought to light my links to several great-grandparents who were free people of color: Stephen Durbin, with wife Celesta Skinner Durbin; Henry Bond, with wife Sophia; Mark Prigg and Sarah; Hazzard Harris and Amelia Prigg Harris; and Russell Hill and Ruth. I learned historical events that linked my family to strategic ways of living amidst laws that imperiled them. Despite laws against free people of color, my family's generations thrived during the antebellum period before the 1860s, with Bonaparte Durbin and wife Grace; Horace Skinner, with wife Hattie Martin Skinner; and Toney Hill. My journey led to the independence of John Gilbert Durbin, with wife Jane, and Moses Martin, with Fanny, and Tower Hill.

I have learned much about the process of researching family history through actual hands-on work. Even though many resources remain to be explored, the discovering of the various documents stimulates my curiosity as to what may be uncovered. I find my interest in uncovering family history has become a consuming obsession, with rewards and treasures of knowledge.

Genealogy triggers vital memories of family that may have receded into the deepest parts of our minds. Old photos, journals, and family mementos wake warm feelings and trigger questions or two that dare to be investigated. The census schedules give us an outline into our family history and may confirm oral stories or answer family questions. As I investigate listings on the census schedules, a picture begins to develop into the background of my family history. Many times the census schedules prompt even more questions, as often they are inaccurate.

My journey continues with confirming family core information in primary documents. Firsthand information is always good to have, but it is not always readily available. Written records—such as diaries, letters, and ledgers—about my family were rare. Not until seeing copies of Social Security applications from my relatives in their own penmanship did I get an actual glimpse into their being. Some certified records can be misleading. Like death records, the information is given by someone else, not always someone close with accurate information that is listed on the certificate. On the other hand, birth certificates are much more reliable. I have learned it is good to confirm family information with multiple primary or secondary documents.

Other documents that have good information are found in our courthouse files and may require references to track down. Land records reveal information and geography. Many of my ancestors had been involved with organizations as trustees and officers, which have been revealed through land records. Not many of my ancestors had a last will and testament, but those who did give me the connections I needed to link my family, which was recorded at the register of wills. The courthouse holds a large variety of legal records to explore.

Like many male relatives, I had to sign up for the selective service by law. These records are future-generation family leads to attain once converted to the archives for research. In the meantime, old military records available at the national archives in Washington, DC, like the WWI and WWII draft records or Civil War enrollment records revealed family information, such as name, age, with place of birth. Even though some military records have no genealogical information, the enlisted name of a relative at least provides evidence of patriotic service by members of our family.

To my surprise, newspaper articles are useful resources that provide a variety of information about events that may include family members. Obituaries are especially valuable. Directories list families within a community with an address.

I learned much about family history during challenging times. For generations, my families were productive free people of color, advancing their race while maintaining a livelihood for family and community. They have been admirable, resilient people who have overcome harsh conditions, including slavery, to build strong communities of integrity and faith.

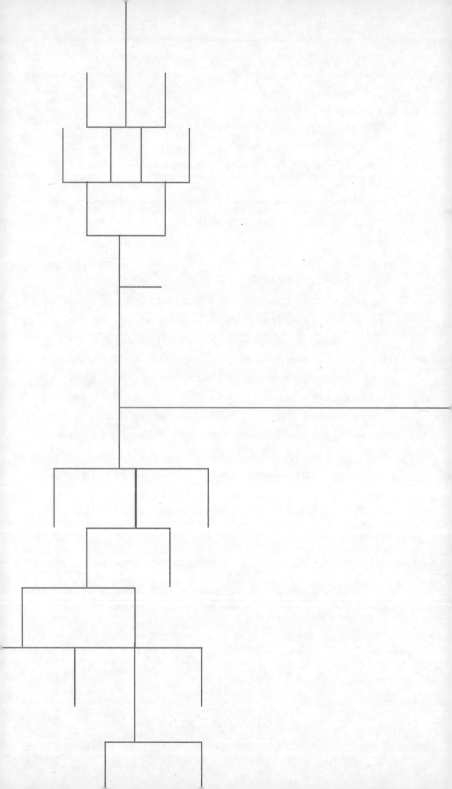

MEETIN'
HOUSE-PLACE
OF WORSHIP

The war promoted tense emotions with uncertainty, much strife, and animosity. I noticed after the war in the 1870 census, many relatives I found before the war I could not find after. I am not sure if they changed names or had an untimely demise. Otherwise, the strength of the faithful remained unmovable as they prayed in the meeting house, while others ventured out to build churches closer to their own homes in surrounding Darlington, Abingdon, and Clarks Chapel and other villages.

Through research, I discovered that the black churches started in the late 1800s in Harford County all, at one point in time, were of the African Methodist Episcopal denomination. According to an annual conference note, churches were developing faster than the bishops could handle, and the lack of support caused many to change to other denominations. The growth was credited to the veteran soldiers returning with vigor and perspective.

I also found in the land records that a church may be of another religious denomination other than AME attended by a black majority; they were often referred to as African, colored, or an AME church. Many churches, like John Wesley in Abingdon and Asbury in Churchville, were in the Methodist Episcopal Church of America, which were supplied by white ministers until the 1860s. Free colored men purchased land to build a place of worship in Abingdon on May 14, 1830 (HD13 folio 300). Isaac Harris, my mother's several-great-grandfather, was one of the founding trustees.

Despite laws prohibiting people of color from congregating without a white authority or overseer, my relatives were very active in establishing churches. On my mom's side, Asbury Methodist land was donated by free people of color, Mary A. Brown and her sister, Melinda, who married Nat Cooper. Even though the church by law was supplied by all white ministers until after the war, it had been faithfully serving the community since 1838. Its first black minister was my several-great-step-grandfather, Henry Matthews.

My church family was the crucial link of the past and central part of who I am today. I compiled the following history from the two sister churches and land records. In 1847, freed men of color purchased land in the city of Havre de Grace for the purpose of building a place of worship for the people of color in the community. I am certain of people of color gathering to meet in central places in secrecy, legally denied the opportunity to organize. Against those odds, certain groups pursued to become a society.

Aquilla Bowser, 49 years old

Charles Barney, 30 years old

John Skinner, 38 years old

William Ramsey, 31years old

Horace Skinner, 46 years old

Henry Hopkins, 35 years old

Recorded and listed on a deed dated October 27, 1847, these six trustees, free men of color, purchased Lot 70 of Square 211, between Adams and Stokes Street, fronting Ontario Street, for five dollars and became the first trustees named on the deed "for the use and benefit of the African church, to build a place of worship."

With the excitement and anticipation of building a place of worship also came peaks of frustration, despair, and disappointment. During this time, a majority of the swampy marshlands of the town were populated by blacks. Havre de Grace's elite and powerful business minority did not allow the building of a place of worship nor a place to congregate. It was illegal for the "African church" to congregate in the heart of the city. Many leaders kept a "Southern-minded view," governed by Southern laws. After two years, through the persistence of the faithful, God answered prayers of the faithful that allowed trustees to purchase land just outside the town line.

Russell Hill, 57 years old

Horace Skinner, 48 years old

Gabriel Christie, 50 years old

Soloman Stuart

John Dutton

Isaac Ross, 55 years old

Samuel Johnson, 57 years old

I discovered a deed that is dated March 17, 1849; for $25.00, these seven men purchased from Richard Barnes and wife Susan (farmers/fisherman) a small lot located next to Chapel Road and Horace Skinner's property with special conditions: (1) "to Bethel Church for the express purpose and use of a meeting house and none other"; and (2) "the right of way of the said road excepted" no public access by law to said property land record HDG35/408 off Chapel Road.

These free people of color, after a year and a half of bitter harassment, with no public access, were only allowed to discreetly meet. I believe, with the help of influential friends, like the Quakers and educated Northern blacks, the church fought back legally. In a detailed indenture recorded September 3, 1850, at the county courthouse, Horace Skinner gave part of his land to trustees "for access to erect or cause to be built a house or place of worship." He incorporated the African Methodist Episcopal Church, authorizing ministers and preachers to use the house or place of worship "to preach and expound God's word therein, all in his desire to promote the temporal spiritual welfare of his colored race" (land record HDG36/268). I believe these faithful met at a huge rock (about 3 by 5 feet) located on this land. In November 2001, while searching for an old cemetery, I discovered this huge rock. I had never seen any like it, and no others of its kind or size were in the area. I could not help but get an overwhelming feeling as I cleared brush from around it. My mind envisioned people of all ages, varying hues of color, free and enslaved gathering around it in the cover of the night to pray, sing, and worship. I could imagine the huge rock as a marked sign to fugitive slaves, letting them know that the nearby water stream led to a safe haven and "Friends" north to freedom. I honor and give tribute to the trustees and the original members who established the all-black church in Harford County.

Aquilla Bowser, 50 years old

Moses Martin, 57 years old

Lewis Martin, 22 years old

William Ramsey

Isaac Dorsey, 33 years old

Oral stories of this first established black church in the area have people of color traveling near and far, walking or by horse and buggy, to the meeting house of worship. As years came, the older members could not travel the distance and started establishing churches near or within their own homes and villages.

In 1857, Russell and Ruth Hill, for $1, incorporated a part of their land to the AME Church of the Eastern Harford Circuit (several churches supplied by one pastor, Rev. Samuel Wilmore; land record ALJ 9/297).

This land will soon become St. James AME Gravel Hill. It is believed that the church first existed since around 1814, when Ebenezer Miller owned the land. It is referred to as the Ebenezer Methodist Episcopal Church or Meeting House. During the 1850s and through the 1860s, there was a rapid growth of blacks purchasing land, especially around Gravelly Hill, as it once was referred to by trustees:

Thomas Miller

Solomon Stuart

William Hill, 65 years old

On March 20, 1864, during the Civil War, the trustees purchased (for $25) more land for a burial ground. Note: Property adjoining to the now-colored Ebenezer Church. The word *now* was underlined on the deed. I can only imagine the church had secretly existed before the AME incorporation (land record WHD15/63).

Thomas Miller

Solomon Stuart

Samuel Johnson

During the Civil War, the church rallied its support and prompted information from AME headquarters, "Mother Bethel," in Philadelphia. Many of our heroic black men walked to Philadelphia, Pennsylvania, to join the Union army. Over 200 black men from Harford County alone fought for their freedom of the colored race. Many were promised freedom to enlist. Many were manumitted, freed to fight. Many free fought for family members who were enslaved. Gravel Hill became a safe haven for black people, slave and free, during the turmoil of war. Gravel Hill was strategically located and somewhat secluded from the beginning of two branches or springs leading into major streams, like Gasheys and Swann Creek, which look over and run into the Chesapeake Bay in Havre de Grace. Along Chapel Road from Bethel Church to Gravel Hill's Ebenezer Church were springs and wooded paths, secluding many family dwellings. In my mind's eye, as I walked the route as a youngster, I could imagine slaves traveling to a safe place, guided possibly by my family members who owned land all along these paths.

I wondered what happened to Bethel AME Church on Chapel Road. "Mt. Zion Meeting House" became its new name, and then it became Mt. Zion AME Church, as noted in a deed dated October 26, 1867, to trustees of the Anderson Institute (WHD19/332), a school for colored people in the city of Havre de Grace, with my grandfather's father's grandfather, Isaac Bishop, as a trustee. At the Maryland Historical Society, I discovered annual conference minutes that state Mt. Zion Church left the conference after the assigned minister ran off with the money, not reporting to the church conference. In the meantime, the faithful members continued to gather in the home of James Peaco Sr. and reestablished and renamed the African Methodist Church, honoring the dedicated Bro. Peaco with two St. James AME churches, Stewartsville (Gravel Hill) and Green Street.

It was a dynamic time for the black faithful at the end of the Civil War. The nation was transformed. Local churches thrived. I have the liberty to worship in these sister churches today and other ones within various communities, and I experience the sense of community and traditional unity founded long ago. What a surprise to have uncovered the family connection of the first-established black church in Harford County, supplied by its own ministers. My research reveals the Bishop family, with Isaac Bishop, Horace Skinner, and Moses Martin for St. James Green Street, and the Bond family, with Russell Hill as trustee and donator of land for Gravel Hill Church.

"Just Making It"

The great stability of my Bishop-Bond's family identity has helped me morally to overcome. Whenever I think I'm barely making it and want to give up, the tracing of my family roots reminded me that I would not be here if my family had not made it. Through my ancestors' collective kindred spirit, I am a survivor.

I read in a biography of ex-slave Frederick Douglass that he escaped through Havre de Grace to Lapidum Ferry on his way north. As the train was dismantled to cross the river, he was assisted possibly by my family members. Can you imagine the city of Havre de Grace with all its congested travelers, including slave catchers, lingering around town? The church was off Chapel Road and led to Earlton Road, which was a direct trail to the ferry in Lapidum into Port Deposit. I can imagine relatives working the ferry boat across the river. Through research, I also discovered people of color owning land along this path. In addition, the free community of Gravel Hill was at the midway point of the trip to cross the river north and on to freedom.

Born into slavery in 1818 in Maryland, Douglass, in the 1840s, escaped from his slave master and moved north into the "Free States" of the Union. Although President Lincoln had not issued his famous Emancipation Proclamation decree, there were more lenient states in the Union for escaped slaves to find refuge. This was not to imply that the original slave owner could not enter; they did usually enter the Free State to reclaim their "property," offering rewards to reclaim them.

Fred Douglass fought his entire life for the rights and liberties of all men, black and white. The color of your skin did not matter to this man who saw through the façade of racism. He led countless marches and rallies aimed at getting the attention of the political forces in the bigger Northern cities.

Policymakers governed according to their own individual opinion in spite of the national body. State by state and, in many cases, locale by locale, laws differed, especially concerning African Americans. Legal interpretations and varying ways of handling certain debated situations made the process even more complicated. Enslaved or free African Americans were at the directive whim of whoever approached them, whether with good or bad intentions. I cannot imagine the state of mind or mood of my ancestors during this period of inconsistent injustice.

I seriously contemplate the sense of trust, or lack of it, throughout the nation and communities in which my ancestors lived. Could people of color rely on the legal system for civil justice? My relatives, along with many other people of color, had to come up with strategies to subvert the biased system and to persevere. Generations today are unable to grasp the legal reality of being someone's property or seeing people regarded as property, like land, horses, or a watch.

One of the first documents I came across at the Historical Society of Harford County was a deed of manumission. Manumissions were a legal document required in the late 1700s into the mid-1800s to release, set free, and liberate from slavery a person of color. This documentation of freedom was recorded as certified proof at the county courthouse that a person was no longer property of another person, even though national laws said otherwise in many states. I can image the struggles to survive and the difficulty in maintaining one's livelihood, not to mention an entire family, with so many against free people of color.

Some law examples are below:

Chapter 66, Laws of Maryland, 1805

The General Assembly of Maryland passed this law to both clearly identify free African Americans and to control the availability of certificates of freedom. These papers were being given to and used by runaway slaves to pass as set free.

Section Six outlined why and how certificates were to be granted to African Americans born free. The certificate describes him or her in detail, including both her maiden and married names, to help prevent someone else from using her certificate. It also indicates that he/she was entitled to freedom because of a manumission or free status of mother. The status of the mother determined the status of her child.

"…Whereas great mischief has arisen from slaves coming into possession of the certificates of free Negroes, by running away and passing as free, under the faith of such certificates: No free Negro or mulatto shall be suffered to keep or carry a fire lock of any kind…without first obtaining a license from the court of the county or corporation in which he resides…"

Chapter 323, Session Laws of Maryland, 1831

The 1831 laws were in reaction to the Nat Turner rebellion. In August of 1831, enslaved people, led by religious slave leader Nat Turner, rebelled against slave owners in Southampton County, Virginia, resulting in the deaths of more than fifty-five white people. After escaping capture for several months, Turner was tried and executed. The scale of this revolt led to many slaves-owning states adopting more stringent laws to control both slaves and free African Americans. Slaveholders and their way of life were being threatened.

"…It shall not be lawful for any free Negro or Negroes, slave or slaves, to assemble or attend any meetings for religious purposes, unless conducted by a white licensed or ordained preacher or some respectable white person…"

Article 66, The Maryland Code: Public General Laws and Public Local Laws, 1860

"…If any person shall have good reason to believe that any free Negro is concerned or engaged in concealing or circulating abolition papers, or furnishing free papers to slaves,…the said justice shall issue a warrant… To search and examine the houses and premises of such a free Negro for abolition or free papers, using as little violence to the feelings of such a free Negro as is compatible with a faithful and diligent search."

—Courtesy of Archives of Maryland Online

A Safe Haven

A few miles north of the town of Havre de Grace, tucked just off the main crossroad to Churchville, was a self-made village called Gravelly Hills. It was a modest community located at the beginning of natural springs and branches that flow through Swan Creek into the Chesapeake Bay. This area was refreshing to me growing up, playing and exploring the forest in this area that was so secure and peaceful. I can see why generations of my family lived their lives and raised families here.

My father's mother was Sarah Bond. Her mother was Amelia Harris, whose parents were Lawson and Margaret Hill-Harris. In 1857, this couple purchased land in Gravel Hill as their home place. In the 1860 census, my family was listed as Lawson Harris, who was age thirty-three years; the family was listed as mulatto laborers, unable to read and write. The land value of his real estate was two hundred dollars, and his personal estate was thirty dollars. Margaret was age thirty-one and unable to read or write with her daughter, Laura V., age four; son Malachi, age two; and son John, three months old. I noticed they were listed directly next door to George Hill, age twenty-five, and wife Anni, age twenty-two. George was a relative of Margaret's.

Pop Lawson Harris and Mom Margaret raised a family and maintained a living to help establish Gravel Hill as a thriving community. Lawson was born a slave, and Margaret was born free, connecting the split within a race of people. On April 28, 1907, at eighty years of age, Lawson Harris died in Havre de Grace. His son Malachi reported on the death certificate that his father was widowed and born to Hazzard Harris and Milly Prigg in Harford County, Maryland. In the 1900 census schedule, Pop Lawson was listed with his second wife, Mary A. Hawkins-Dorsey, fifty-eight years old, and her sister, Annie M. The spelling of his name was "Losson T.," age seventy-six; he was born in July 1823 and married fifteen years.

My exploration into the life of family members became very interesting as the search got deeper into the past. I soon would find out that Lawson was the son of extraordinary parents. His parents were listed, on his death certificate, as Hazzard Harris and Milly Prigg—both of Harford County. I noticed right away the unusual names. Could Lawson have been named for the lawful son of espoused parents? Marriage of people of color had not been recorded at the county courthouse before the 1860s. The mainstream society of that generation, for the most part, did not recognize the marriage of African Americans but reaped the benefits of a fruitful union. The benefit of human mass production in many cases was encouraged by those who considered people of color property for profit.

My investigation had not recovered a marriage certificate for Pop Lawson and Mom Margaret. I can assume village rituals within close-knit communities, like "jumping the broom," were the custom for public matrimony. Around the mid-1850s, Margaret's father had been heavily involved as trustee of the church near Havre de Grace for some time. Even though these church records are nonexistent, it's quite possible the couple married in a traditional religious setting. Another possibility could be with the friends, Quakers, who were prominent throughout the area, especially Darlington, where Lawson's parents lived. His second marriage was recorded among the court records on February 8, 1884. At the age of about fifty-three years old, as a widower, he married Mary Dorsey, age forty-nine years old, a widow in Darlington, by Minister John D. Cox.

Pop Lawson and Mom Margaret had about ten children between the years of 1854 and 1872, partly during the height of the Civil War. I can envision this family oblivious to the nation's turmoil and being busy with their lives within the confines of a close-knit community, a safe haven. This couple maintained a livelihood within the secured, tranquil setting of the home place in their family-surrounded village freely. Pop Lawson, a former slave, had been aware firsthand of the crucial issues of the war as neighbors walked to join the colored troops in Philadelphia and the atmosphere of liberation for those enslaved as he once was a few years earlier. People of color were collectively concerned about the plight and insecurity of their race in Maryland, a border state with resident Southern sympathizers and slave owners.

Lawson's death certificate lists his parents as Hazzard Harris and Amelia Prigg, notable Harford County residents. On August 18, 1899, the local newspaper reported:

"Oldest Woman in Maryland"

Aunt Milly Harris said to have been 121 years old.

Aunt Milly Harris, a venerable colored woman, died at the home of her daughter, Keziah Bond, in Darlington, on Friday August 11th, at the reputed age of 121 years. She was born and passed her entire life in Harford County; she formerly belonged to the Gilbert family, who lived upon the property near Churchville, now owned by Charles James.

According to the statement of her grandson William Harris, who is employed with Flower's Livery Stable, Bel Air. She was emancipated sixty-eight years ago. Her oldest child, George Harris, was born when she was seventeen years of age, and he is now 103 years old. Two other children, Haviland Harris, age sixty-eight, and Keziah Bond, age sixty-six years, are still living. Aunt Milly enjoyed unusually good health during her long life, having been sick but twice in the past twenty years. She was buried on Sunday at Hosanna Church, near Darlington.

This newspaper article gave me crucial clues to further investigate the Harris links in my Bishop and Bond family. It states Mom Millie was emancipated sixty-eight years ago, by the Gilbert family, where she was born and raised near Churchville. Lawson would have been about three years old, based on his death certificate and census schedules. The newspaper article does not mention Lawson as one of Millie's children. I believe he could not physically travel due to debilitating health issues, which caused paralysis stated at his death. Based on Mom Millie's newspaper tribute, the information sparks my search for freedom papers.

I have learned discrepancies and inaccuracies were not just in the past but also made in the present. Errors in spelling, age, and other data were common in transcribing. The Internet, websites, and publications should be a reference directly to the primary documents of where the information can be confirmed. I have found more details in original records than in indexes, which have helped reveal more leads and enrich my family roots.

Freedom papers connect people of color to slavery, whether by attaching them to another person or providing legal proof of their freedom. Pop Lawson's mother, Milly, was owned by the Gilbert family in Churchville. I looked for them in connection with her and found many references. At the Historical Society, indexed files guided me to freedom papers and the booklet *Hunter Sutherland's Slave Manumissions and Sales in Harford County, Maryland, 1775-1865*, which directed me to others, like the following: "Freed by Elizabeth Coale, any issues, at age thirty years of age, paid thirty dollars by Negro Milly, age twenty-nine. Moses, age eight; Rachael, age five; George, age five; Lawson, age three; and Eliza, age three years."

Pop Lawson would be free at age thirty in the year 1857, according to this document of his mother purchasing her children from slavery. I can see the secrecy of having children before the official freedom date being an issue. Slaves bore slave children and the confusion of being free or not when set to a particular date. How would they have known, not being able to read or write without relying on those under their control? Pop Lawson and Mom Margaret Harris had their first child before 1857, but with her being free, I trust it was not challenged nor an issue in the comforts within a safe haven of the home place.

A VISION WITH VALUES

An era or generation of time is often defined as every four-teen to twenty-two years. One era often overlaps into the next generational era. For instance, the Gilded Era was cut off by the period of the Civil War, which, at its end, wel-comed an era of social cooperativeness with its missionaries. These moments and periods in history define what America would become. With this transition, many unique changes occurred. The way things had always been was no more. The abolishment of slavery, an idea only dreamed of and talked about, came into fruition. A sentiment many hoped, wished, and prayed for was finally a reality.

The dawn of a new day brought exuberance and shouts from the countless souls involved in the cause of freedom. Many knew not how to live free and were faced with uncer-tainties. Former slaves were left exposed to the complex, entwined components of an established governmental sys-tem with little knowledge. Free people of color learned to rely on one another for survival from generation to genera-tion. On the other hand, newly released former slaves, espe-cially the old, were thrust into an unknown area of complete independence after centuries of undignified indoctrination.

The period directly after the American Civil War established freedmen's communities, incorporating institutions of education, training, and spiritual support. The Bishop-Bond family was instrumental in contributing to the advancement of the community. Having been free years, Isaac Bishop was well-established within his town. On the other hand, the Harry Bond family lived near Peach Bottom, Pennsylvania, just over the Mason-Dixon Line.

The 1860 census schedule lists Isaac Bishop, age forty-five, carpenter; Rachel, age forty, unable to read or write; Jacob, age twelve; and Charles, age seven. Their personal estate was valued at two hundred dollars. The 1860 census year was the last to have a separate schedule with names of slave owners listing the age, gender, and race of a slave. In 1850 and 1860, separate schedules had columns to check if a slave was a fugitive, manumitted, and deaf-blind-dumb, and they also listed how many slave houses the owner had. Despite having slaveholders, Maryland, a border state, had one of the largest free-people-of-color populations among all the states. It was estimated that between 1780 to the 1860, the African American population grew from a quarter to more than fifty percent free. Upon finding my Bishop family in the free census schedules, I continued to search more into documents of the past at the local historical society.

Throughout American history, debates occurred on every aspect of the lives of people of color, free and enslaved. Laws were constructed, ratified, and applied in regard to various groups. The laws concerning those of African descent were overwhelmingly numerous within each jurisdiction. Regulating servants began upon the arrival of ships with slaves to Jamestown in 1619. Maryland's initial laws concerned indentured servants in general without regard to race but escalated to more stringent laws specifically related to Negroes, those of African descent in 1715—for example "No Negros by being baptized shall have any more right to freedom than before." Baptism was a major rite and initiation to be civilized by Christian colonists at this time. Particular emphasis on the Negro limited proprietary advances, setting apart this specific race of people.

My research continues tracing family roots in court records. At the Historical Society, I discovered a file of names indexed to specific documents. Within several papers, the first was a Certificate of Freedom, with "Negro Isaac Bishop" underlined in bold, centered letters. It reads:

Negro Isaac Bishop
aged about forty-one years, very dark complexion,
about five feet five and three quarters inches high,
a small scar upon the right eyebrow and another on
the right wrist, a high forehead, and has a pleasant expression of countenance whenever spoken
to, became free by virtue of a deed of manumission
from one Henry Barnes on the 17th of
November 1854
Identified by Chas H. Bouldin & pap, appeared on
the 6th of January 1855
A. L. Jarret, clerk
State of Maryland, Harford County

I was overjoyed to have read this freedom paper, which identified my direct generational ancestor fifth grandfather, or grandfather's father's grandfather, with a high forehead and pleasant countenance. My trail to tracing family history proceeded to the mentioned deed. A deed of manumission was signed, sealed, and recorded by the justice of peace in the county court. This descriptive paper was an identity-card free people of color had to carry, like we carry our driver's license today.

Within the courthouse, various transactions in regard to African Americans both free and enslaved are documented. Many of the records label a person of color as Negros, colored, mulatto, African, or black. Some free persons' full names with ages and relatives are listed, while most enslaved persons are listed by first name only.

The documentation of family vital information varies from generation to generation. In my research, I found that present-day generations generally form more data than preceding ones. Today, in tracing family roots, many repositories provide searchable indexes. For instance, most census schedules can be searched online and become available to the public seventy-two years after it was taken. The 1940 census became public in 2012. An archive of documents located in a variety of files at the historical society reveals a treasure trove of family records. To my surprise, I uncovered a bill of sale connecting to my family, stating:

> Whereas Stephen Jones in his lifetime sold to
> Isaac Bishop his Negro woman named Rachel
> for the sum of two hundred dollars and received
> a portion of the purchase money. Therefore and
> whereas since the death of the said Stephen Jones,
> the said Isaac has paid me the sum of one hundred
> & twenty dollars, being the balance of the said
> purchase money and interest. To wit.

> A. L. Jarret

Recorded within a very short period of time, Pop Isaac, on November 17, was legally discharged from slavery. A few months later, on January 6, 1855, age forty-five, he was descriptively identified with a Certificate of Freedom. On January 20, 1855, Pop Isaac paid in full the balance of the purchase price of his Negro woman, Rachel, about forty years old. It's just as close to a marriage certificate for people of color and former slaves during the antebellum era in a Southern slave state. Remarkably, I later went through the land records, where I recovered the fact that Isaac Bishop purchased land in Harford County.

> On November 8, 1855 Isaac Bishop purchased the parcel lot #10, called "The Stokes Four Acre Lot," located between Stokes and Water Streets in the city of Havre de Grace, Maryland, for the price of one hundred and fifty dollars in hand (ALJ no.7 folio 6). January 1, 1856, Isaac Bishop took out a three hundred and forty-six dollar mortgage (ALJ no.7 folio7).

Locating these papers was a learning experience for me in the fact that, in my mind, I have been in connection with the process people of color went through in obtaining their freedom. I realized Pop Isaac had shown courtesy through his pleasant countenance as he sought to achieve the vision of family freedom and land ownership. Extraordinary is the value of his legacy freely given by him to me, generation to generation.

I can imagine Pop Isaac as a carpenter during his lifetime, honing his skills within the growing town's homes and buildings. I cannot help but think of my uncles, my father's brothers, building their own homes, remodeling other homes, repairing and renovating structures as needed. We could say it's a gift or even a driven passion, but without a doubt, the "Isaac" within them, natural yet God-inspired through kinship by divine ordination, is a link passed on to generations.

The census reveals that within the close-knit neighborhood was a diverse group of diligent people of different ethnic backgrounds who were hardworking and able to provide a sufficient livelihood to provide for their family. Tireless like Isaac, his close neighbors worked as merchants, shoemakers, blacksmiths, and laborers. Many around him were foreign-born from Germany, Switzerland, Prussia, and Ireland. While they individually lived to raise a family, each one collectively made major contributions to the building, upkeep, and growth of an ever-moving small town.

Now, as I compile the pieces of my family history, I am reminded of my childhood, playing along the banks of the Susquehanna River. I had taken for granted all the old things around me, not realizing their connection, history through kinship, which reveals an obvious generational link. I have taken another look back at my research.

My grandfather's father's grandfather, Isaac Bishop, was enslaved and then freed; he provided for family and worked and owned land among the railroads, canals, and structures, which today are rusty relics, mere remnants, and a trace of generations long gone. In every sense, I admire Pop Isaac's courteous and loyal advancement, especially for himself, our family, the community, and his people as a free person of color.

One night as I browsed the Internet, I came across a genealogical blog, which also was printed in the local genealogical society newsletter. This inquiry was from a lady from my hometown looking for information about a black man named Isaac Bishop. I replied, and she told me that "ole man Isaac Bishop" was mentioned in an old wildlife publication with renowned duck decoy carver Samuel Barnes of Havre de Grace. It is quite possible because the connection with the Barnes family was definitely there. Not only were several Barnes families as among his neighbors, but it was Henry Barnes who discharged the highly respected Isaac from slavery. A testimony of dedication, stability, and loyalty within a small close-knit community was proven in the working together of these two families.

At the local library, I viewed the 1870 census schedules on microfilm. Despite the viewer being somewhat difficult to see and maneuver, in time I found my Isaac Bishop family. He was listed age fifty-one, with Rachel's age forty-five; Sarah Ushin, age twenty-three; George, age ten; and Mary, age eight.

I had to keep in mind the inconsistent ages throughout this period in history. In most cases, the majority of people could not read, write, or keep an accurate count. During the antebellum generation, in many areas, it was illegal for women and people of color to read or write. This greatly added to disparities in age, status, name spelling, and, in some cases, type of race. Substantiation of facts was not always possible, especially in tracing African American roots. Its history in many cases comes to a specialized, speculative hypothesis.

In the 1860 census, within Isaac's household were two sons, Jacob and Charles. I have not found additional records of them as of yet, but in 1870, Sarah was listed as "M" for mulatto, which was the name describing a person of mixed race, presumably African American and Caucasian. Taken in within Isaac and Rachel Bishop's household, the census schedule columns checked off are that she and both parents were of foreign birth. Sarah Usher was listed as being born in the West Indies. George and Mary were both listed with the letter *B* for "black," with column twelve checked for "mother of foreign birth." So I speculate that these are her children, born to a foreign mother and African American father, since column eleven is not checked for "father of foreign birth." Within a few years, in 1873, my grandfather's father, Augustus Bishop, was born and raised by grandparents Isaac and Rachel in Havre de Grace.

Mom Rachel, the supportive wife and grandmother, was listed in the census with Pop Isaac. Before I discovered the freedom papers in the court records, I made my first trip to the state archives in Annapolis. It was overwhelming. I planned an all-day outing, not knowing what to expect. I arrived very early, before they unlocked the door. It was as if I was entering a secured building in that I had to present ID, sign in, and place my personals items in a locker. Upon waiting permission to enter the huge library area, I was asked to make sure I signed in to use the microfilm and sign in at the desk. People were watching me from the corners of their eyes as I walked in awe throughout, not knowing where to start. I suppose the stares were toward me for looking like a lost puppy. Finally, a lady offered to help by giving me a quick tour. In the microfilm room, I had to sign for a viewing machine, which I was third in line to use.

The files were cataloged by Soundex number. A man gave me a formula to convert my last name into a number that matched all surnames that sounded or spelled close to mine. I spent all that time figuring to come up with a three-digit number that is on my driver's license. Time had gone by, and they said we all had to leave the building for an hour lunch. Disappointed, I went to my car to eat my packed lunch, anxious to research, which I had not done yet.

When I went through the process of signing in all over again, I realized I had no idea of how to use the microfilm machine. A lady said someone would help. I found film on death certificates, thinking I could find something. It was my turn to get a machine, and there were no helpers around. I did not want to disturb others who were quietly working with their heads down. I sat in front of one of the huge machines and stared at it. Another man researching nearby saw me perplexed and offered to help. He showed me how to place the film in and work the projector. I was moving in my search and had gone through two cartridges before timed out to re-sign in to use a viewer. Thank goodness there were machines available with no wait time. I sat down to view, and I found Rachel Bishop. I jumped with glee, hardly containing myself. It was so quiet. I think I said "Yes" so loudly that a lady came over to say they would be closing in ten minutes. I thought, *Oh no!* and asked about getting a copy. She made me a copy of the front and back of the certificate of death, which stated:

Rachel Bishop
Died in Havre de Grace, Harford County,
Maryland
1899; month 8; day 23; age 86
Female; colored; widow; number of children living:
-0-
Wife of Isaac Bishop
Cause of death—old age
No medical attendant
Information given by a grandson

Mom Rachel and Pop Isaac Bishop lived long lives in Havre de Grace with family and community friends. Research continues to link where they further connect family lines. Their grandson Augustus links the generations through his son, my grandfather Oscar, with my father George and me, his son.

Cousin Connections

"You kids are related to all…"

It is said the further back in one's family roots you go, you're bound to come across a common relative. As I research into preceding generations, the family links intertwine with many lines and branches of my family tree. My research has only been in the same county thus far. I thought it would take me to another region sooner, but it hasn't. My journey has been extraordinary in the county. So it does not surprise me to find distant cousins not knowing their relation and marrying one another over time.

Mom Celesta Durbin-Bishop, direct connection to Bonaparte, the son of John Gilbert Durbin, links several cousins throughout Harford County. His daughter, Isabella

Durbin-Kennard, connects my mother's family directly. She married Peter Kennard and had mulatto twins at age forty-one. In 1845, John Thomas and Hanna were born. John was awarded to the Orphans Court in 1860, stating both parents as dead, and he, as an apprentice, was to farm under John Bailey. Pop John T. Kennard served in the Civil War USCT.

Upon his return home, John T. Kennard married Harriet Hamilton and lived in Churchville, Maryland. They raised two children near the Asbury Church. Alverta was born in 1868; she married Jerome Harris, son of Hazzard T. Harris. David R. Kennard was born in 1870; he married Mami R. Butler, the daughter of Annie Harris-Butler, the daughter of Isaac Harris and Elizabeth A. Lingham.

Pop David and Mom Mami Kennard raised thirteen kids; my mother's mother was the eleventh child. Mom-Mom Hattie E. married Pop-Pop Albert C. Lewis and raised nine children. Two of their daughters married into the Bishop family—my mother, Anne (George), and her eldest sister, Grace (Eugene). The union interlinks generations and cousins of the Bishop-Bond family.

If this isn't entangled enough, my mother's father's grandfather, Robert Lewis, married a Millie Bond in 1921. It is believed that my mother's father's mother's mother was a Bond. Research is still pending on many of these cousins and relatives.

The Bond connection was throughout Harford County; founders of the county and early settlers were the Bond family. It was not a surprise growing up to discover a main road in Bel Air named Bond Street.

As I followed the census schedule as a guide to my Bond family, I realized how many parents used the same first names. The task of matching my family to that which was listed became time consuming and impossible. Another approach had to be added in assisting the assorting of the many Bond families in Harford County alone. I just think the nicknames and alternates within a one-family unit were tremendous and not always recorded.

Pop George Bond's father was named William Henry or Harry Bond; in searching with discrepancies in age, I found several with those variations in names. Nonetheless, further examination of land records, wills, court papers, and other freedom papers match the family and area in which they lived. Land records place the William and Sophia Bond family in Dublin. I believe these are the parents of Henry, Tower, and many other siblings grouped by area of the Bond family as free people of color. In an archive document, a young Henry was hired to supply musical entertainment by playing the violin.

In 1832, the sheriff had to list free blacks in the county by order of a Maryland law. It included a head count by name, age, and sex of those free people of color who might be willing to be removed out of the state of Maryland to possibly Liberia in Africa.

Harford County had preserved its list, and copies are available. The original copy located at the state archives was the most accurate by family units. There was listed a twenty-six-year-old Heny next to Tower, age twenty-one years old. Heny and Tower were grouped with Ben, thirty-eight; Ned, twenty-one; George, fourteen; and Lewis, twelve. There were many more Bond family members listed throughout to be examined in family groups, like Henry, forty-four; Ben, twenty-eight; Ben, fifteen; Westley, nine; and Freeborn, two.

Pop William Henry "Harry" Bond was twenty-six years of age on this list from 1832. Pop Harry was the son of Henry and Sophia Bond, living near Darlington, Maryland, in the 1850 census. I am yet to locate his wife's death certificate, Mom Sarah A. E. Bond, last listed in the 1920 census at age eighty-six. They started their family in Pennsylvania near Peach Bottom but returned to a close-knit family in Harford County, Maryland, as free people of color.

In 1832, there were more than sixteen-hundred free people of color listed by the sheriff of Harford County. As I look over this list to find members of the Bishop-Bond family, I located several Bond surnames and not one with the Bishop last name. In my research, the Bond family members connected with Harris, Prigg, and Hill families were freed before 1832. Curiously, on the Bishop line of family, Martin and Gilbert were also listed and found thus far in my research.

Interestingly on this list, I carefully noted the family groups and names. Mom Celesta Durbin-Bishop's forefather was Bonaparte. I thought that was an unusual name that would stand out on any list. I remember the freedom document from John Durbin, releasing and setting free his children in 1815, and I matched several first names. To my amazement, the surname was different for the group of names who matched my Durbin family. John, age seventy-two, was listed with the last name Gilbert, with Jane, age fifty; Bonaparte, age twenty-five; Isabella, age twenty-eight; and Christian, age twenty-two. So I searched for an answer to confirm whether or not this was my family. Ironically, they are listed close to Pop Moses Martin, age forty, and Pop Towney Hill, age seventy; son Pop Russell Hill, age forty; with wife Mom Ruth, age forty. Within this close-knit village and community of free people of color, it would be natural to suppose that these great-grandparents of my Bishop-Bond family knew each other, linking community. I cannot help but think they had a family connection somewhere within the generational tier.

I found in the land records John Durbin Gilbert purchasing three and a quarter acres from John Pybus on June 1, 1811, for twenty-four dollars and thirty-seven-and-a-half cents (land record HD W folio186).

Harford County,
Be it remembered that on the fifth
day of June 1811 personally appeared before two of
the justices of the peace for said county the within
named John Pybus and acknowledged the within
instrument of writing to be his act and deed and
the bargained land and premises therein mentioned
and described to be the right and estate of the
within named John Durbin Gilbert his heirs and
assigns forever.
Acknowledged before
Wm Smith
James Stephenson
Rec'd June the first 1811 of the within named John
Durbin Gilbert the sum of twenty-four dollars and
thirty-seven and a half cents, it being the valuable
consideration for the bargained land and premises
within mentioned and described.
Rec'd me John Pybus
Test Wm Smith

I noticed this legal document was certified by two county officials, justices of the peace, whose names appear on another land deed acquired by Pop John Durbin Gilbert. In 1829, for one hundred sixty-six dollars and eighty-nine cents, he purchased forty-one acres from Herman Stump. This land deed was recorded in the courthouse under HD 12 folio407 and certified by W. Smith and J. Worthington. This land was adjacent to property owned by James Stephenson, justice of peace, on the 1811 deed. I believe these official men to be neighborhood friends who knew and lived near my family.

On November 4, 1837, the equity courts sold at public auction to Henry Barnes to settle a family dispute four lots property of the late Jack Durbin, sometimes called John Gilbert, which was recorded in land record HD24 folio158. This confirms they are one and the same person. Bonaparte, his son, was mentioned as executor of his will, which I viewed at the Register of Wills and requested a copy of the inventory of his estate from the Maryland State Archives, which equally distributes his estate to his nine surviving children.

Grace Wilson, Hannah Hopkins, Susan Giles, Harriet Wesley, Mary Presbury, Isabella Kennard, Bonaparte Durbin, Eliza Young, and Christian Durbin were all free people of color, linking generations to Jack Gilbert Durbin.

I retrieved copies of some of my Durbin family's descriptive freedom papers. Descendant cousins continued to live near Hopewell, close to Gravel Hill and near the property purchased by John "Jack" Gilbert Durbin in 1811. Many of his children were described in the following freedom papers.

Christian Durbin
Age about forty-seven years, dark complexion,
about five feet, eight inches in height and has a scar
on the left wrist, is free and became free by virtue

of a deed of manumission executed by John Durbin
on the 28th of March 1815, records in Liber HD
no Y folio 266 one of the land records of
Harford County
Identified by Samuel Magain
this 10th day of August 1857
A. L. Jarret clk

Negro Elizabeth Young
State of Maryland
Harford County
I, Henry Dorsey Clerk,
of Harford County Court, the same being a court
of record, hereby certify that the bearer hereof,
Negro Elizabeth Young, formerly Elizabeth
Durbin, about thirty-four years of age, rather
dark complexion, about five feet six inches high,
slight, slender built, with her front teeth very much
decayed and having scar on the outer side of
her left wrist occasioned by possible burn, is now
free and became free by virtue of a deed
of manumission duly executed on the 28th day
of March 1815 by a certain John Durbin and
recorded in Liber HD no. Y folio 266 one of
the Land Record Books of Harford County
Court. In testimony whereof, I
subscribe my name and
affix the seal of Harford County
Court this 10th day of May 1842
Identified by John Mahan
Henry Dorsey clk

Negro Susan
Maryland Harford County

Hereby certify that the bearer here of
Negro Susan, thirty-two years of age, five feet,
two inches high, dark complexion,
has a considerable scar on the upper
part of the breast, occasioned from a burn, has
a pleasant countenance and was born free and
raised
in Harford County.

In testimony whereof, I have
hereto subscribed my name and
affixed the seal of Harford County
Court this thirteenth day of May, eighteen
hundred and thirty-two
Identified by Asaal Bailey
Henry Dorsey elk

Negro Hannah Hopkins
State of Maryland Harford County to wit
I, Henry Dorsey, clerk of Harford County Court,
the same being a court of record, hereby certify that
the bearer here of Negro Hannah Hopkins, formerly Hannah Durbin, about forty-eight years of
age. Slender-made woman, five feet, six and a half
inches high, and of light complexion is free and
became free by virtue of a deed of manumission
from John Durbin, bearing date 28th March 1815
and duly executed acknowledge and recorded in
Liber HD no Y folio 266 one of the Land Record
Books of Harford County Court

In testimony & c this 10th day of May 1842
Henry Dorsey clk

Identified by Jno Mahan
Mulatto Harriot
State of Maryland, Harford County Court
I hereby certify that the bearer hereof, mulatto
Harriot, five feet, four and a half inches high,
twenty-one years of age and of a light complexion,
became free at the age of sixteen years, in virtue of
a deed of manumission executed by John Durbin
of said county, duly executed and recorded amongst
the land records of Harford County Court.
The said mulatto Harriott has a scar on her small
finger on the right hand, a mole on her neck, has
a black mark or spot on the left arm near the
place where she was vaccinated, and has a scar
under right arm and was raised partly in Harford
County and partly in Chester County. In testimony
whereof, I have here unto set my hand and affixed
that seal of my office this 22nd day of June 1819.

Identified by Amos Gilbert
Henry Dorsey, clk

Enslavement

As the state of being under the control of something or controlled by another person, the institution of slavery was much more than persons being another individual's personal property. The mind-set to justify its degrading act was to say that the Negro races were less than human. We hear of the inhumane actions implicated throughout generations of those enslaved, but can we truly grasp what this system had done to a race of people? Physically, emotionally, and culturally, slavery marked forever people of color with psychological consequences yet unresolved today. Will one race ever accept the differences of another without demeaning the other? Not when there are subjective gain, power, and inferiority advantages. Today I believe our society has redefined slavery. It's still about the monetary gain, but the approach to get it is through the use of subliminal images, control, and chemical addictions at the expense of those who fall prey into it. Enslavement is more than a collective system; it's a disease intertwined in life, affecting the body, the mind, and the spirit of those it has in its grips.

I refuse to be enslaved to shame, frustration, and self-pity. In our complex world, we are influenced by people, situations, and material items. The social moment of the majority persuades us to believe they are doing the right thing. After years of waiting, I now have a new smart phone with the latest technology. I was persuaded it would help ease my business travels. After several months of learning, it still baffles me. Clear out of the blue, it talks, and I have not figured out how to stop it, other than turning it off. I barely use it. Without a doubt, because of who I am, I will investigate and personally ask someone about the features I've yet to use. I am influenced by the technology, but it does not strip me of who I am. It will only advance what I can do and who I can be.

Unlike the dilemma of using my smartphone, even more serious events in life influence who we are and what we become. I often ask why bad things seem to happen when you try your best to do well. In 1994, I lived in Baltimore, worked two full-time jobs, volunteered, and traveled home to attend church every weekend. The year had been turbulent from the beginning. My father had a stroke a few years earlier, and the family was dealing with his recovery and flipped personality. He was not mentally the same. The kind, likable person had become mean and nonsocial, lashing out at whomever, whenever he needed to vent. My mom took the brunt of the verbal lashings as she balanced working and taking care of a younger cousin. I would give my father attention by driving him around with me to the post office, park, and back to my aunt's to stay periodically. My father took my brother's sudden death hard as he dealt with internal problems and health issues himself.

My brother died just before Memorial Day as a result of a self-inflicted wound he suffered while breaking in to a local store. He had bled out and was found lying along the main road toward the house. My mom was driving and taking care of business that morning when she had recognized partial clothing as my brother lay lifeless, covered, and surrounded by authorities. She spoke to my father, and they both stayed home waiting in disbelief and shock.

That day at my accounting job, I was unable to get enough blood to check my blood sugar. All day it seemed a struggle for no reason. In the afternoon, my office listens to the news and traffic reports before leaving. The news did not say any names, but I told a coworker something was wrong; that report felt strange. Certain people, at times, have a spiritual connection or psychic sense, especially regarding those with a close relationship. It is an innate sense, which lets the conscience know of trouble in some way, above all when not in direct communication with one another. At 5p.m, routinely I left and went to my night job at the restaurant I had worked in about four years. I had not yet changed my shirt, and the phone rang. It was my mom, who rarely calls. She could barely speak. Not allowing her to utter a word, I said, "I'm on my way home."

I immediately left to join her and my father. The detectives had visited with a photo of my lifeless brother earlier that afternoon, confirming what she had already known. It defies human logic at times, surpassing physical and verbal communication in ways we cannot explain but by intuition strongly sensed. We are not sure if his desire to do what he did was influenced by the strains of others or if he was enslaved to a powerful addiction of his own doing. No matter what the influences were, he made one unfortunate choice, which instantly ended his life.

No one truly knows what another person has to cope with, go through, or truly deal with in their life. Living with diabetes and dealing with financial disappointments, I often wonder why bad things happen to good people. Over time, I have realized it's to strengthen our spirit in faith through life's struggles and each challenge. Sometimes those bad things test our endurance to a breaking point. I am sensitive to the lives succumbed to the pressures of slavery. History had not recorded their names, but I suppose a countless number of lives had not survived its demeaning grips. What I have gone through does not compare to what they had gone through.

In the late 1980s to the mid-1990s, I worked tirelessly to fill my time and obligations. My family experienced a considerable loss of members on both my parents' sides. I had gone to so many funerals that I was desensitized to mourning. To cope, I started a journal to God about what I was feeling and doing to deal with my grieving. I kept busy with all that I did while singing and praying more earnestly, incorporating daily devotions into all that I did throughout my daily routine. With time come many changes in our lives, like loss of loved ones, mental turmoil, and pain from disappointments of others. Time is relentless in our aging bodies and debilitating health. With a steady beat, the years move on, and we accept what changes may be. I believe the passing of time is heavenly sent to cure and heal my emotional sorrows. "Earth has no sorrow which heaven cannot heal."

God puts people in your life to help in times of difficulty when you think you may break. Slavery was economically profitable to some but separated people from their racial culture, class, and family. During these times, enslavement not only disconnected people from their identity but physically and emotionally separated them from who they were. The little sense of community and family during slave times in many cases had been redefined. I can imagine secret gatherings late at night amongst the comfort and support of loved ones. Family is an intimate bond that is not easily replaced. Family is a unique and divine bond that God Almighty has ordained. This common bond, with its vital links, keeps us as individuals from breaking and withdrawing from who we are.

Often a feeling of "Why me?" gets into my thoughts when bad things happen to me. *Why do I have diabetes? Why so many financial struggles?* And if it's not one thing, it's another. My self-pity and questions of "why" had not come into play when I was humiliated. I have kept this following incident to myself for years before revealing what almost brought forth a part of who I am not. I had to have an intimate talk with someone close about what I was holding within. I contemplated talking with my father, but he had a stroke and was too fragile to console me. I really needed someone else outside of the professionals I had been seeing week after week for more than a year to release within an angry inner need to do something. I found counsel in a cousin, my father's first cousin on his mother's side, William Bond, or "Billy."

We had a special connection as family, but we both also were ordained ministers in our growing family church. With my father going through his illness, Billy was an ideal father I could talk with and confide in for consolation. Despite all he and his wife Betty went through, they had a welcoming home, especially for young people, as they successfully raised seven children and a nephew. I felt at home and safe and secure in their extra room, as if it were my own.

I told him I had been cruising the dangerous streets of Baltimore City, intermingling and having a conversation with guys who I thought could direct me to a hit man. I was sprung into doing something after a year of weekly counsel with a Christian therapist and monthly visits to a psychologist's office to talk and answer questions of "How did that make you feel?" For months I had a feeling of revenge that had been brought about by constant talk and remembering my traumatic experience with paid professional strangers. Whether or not these feelings had initially been coated by shock, I was not sure why I felt the buildup of anger many months later.

At first cousin Billy thought I was joking, but he soon realized I wasn't. I went on to tell him I almost purchased a gun the night before in the streets. The guy had it in his hand, showing it to me because I had asked about getting one. He was going to sell it to me for two hundred dollars. Yes, I had been talking and asking about a hit man and then buying a gun for months, but finally the reality struck me like a bolt of lightning. When I saw that short, steel weapon, I freaked out. I was beyond myself for even talking about it. I had never seen anything like it in my life—a gun that kills! I tried to keep my composure and told the guy it was not what I was looking for and quickly drove home.

The realization of seeing a weapon of death, however, did not deter my inner desire for revenge, an emotion that enslaved me. At this point, I knew cousin Billy could not believe what I was telling him. He wanted to know who, why, and what had me so totally out of character. He knew I was not a person to pursue illicit, troublesome activities and be near any of it. Someone or something can influence who you are in many ways by controlling your physical and emotional environment consistently or in one gripping moment in time.

My cousin had known all about my working two full-time jobs during the week and my coming home to attend church every weekend. He also knew of my ongoing volunteer service with the Buddy Program and how I met my buddy client, Grady, at church. I had been in constant contact via phone with Grady, and in between jobs, occasionally I would visit him in his apartment. One night, after working at the Italian carryout, I took him some food. I had told him over the phone earlier I would treat him to a nice home-made meatball sub to cheer him up. He had told me he was moving into a hospice care home in the next few weeks and needed help to pack up and move a few things.

Upon my arrival, Grady and I greeted each other with the same hug and smile, and I gave him the sub as we proceeded to talk. He had company that night whom I had never met. As I excused myself to go home, Grady asked if I could drop his company off on my way. I had no reason not to, and I knew Grady for years. So I agreed to honor my buddy's request.

Grady's company was a very quiet guy dressed in what looked like a deep-blue uniform. I would say his clothes looked like those of a police training cadet, security person, or the like. He was well built, about six feet, with a thick, smooth frame and short hair. I tried to make conversation with him, but he only gestured with an inaudible "yeah" and "right." As we got in my car, he said his name was Johnson. I asked him where he lived.

He said, "Down this street a few blocks," and he looked back nervously.

As I drove my car not too far from Grady's apartment on St. Paul Street, we passed by the railroads of Penn Station, and he directed me to turn left, passing a club with a live band playing music loudly. I remember saying, "You live over here?"

He said, "Close by," and he told me to continue down a rocky road lined with warehouses. In the middle of nowhere, he said firmly, "Pull over and stop right here." Johnson seemed no longer quiet or nervous as he looked at me directly and said, "Get out."

I could not move or say anything. He opened the door and exploded with body gestures, as if he was going to hit me, but with one strong blow, he stabbed my car's steering wheel with a huge hunter's knife. Instantly, I thought he had stabbed me but did not. I said, "What you want? I have little money. You want my car?"

He said, "No. Get out the car."

I did not know what to think. I put the car in gear, pressed on the gas, and he clutched the gear and shut it off somehow. Even though I still had my seat belt on, he snatched me out of my seat, dragging me through the passenger side into a dark, wooded area.

I was already in shock, as I could not believe what was happening to me. He was twice my size and had a strong, one-handed grip on me. I could not move as I felt tree branches scrape me. My head was pressed against the thick side of his stomach when I felt one hand down the back, inside of my pants. In the distance, I heard the sounds of train horns blowing and the engines going over the tracks. I remember excruciating pain as my body was partially on a dead tree stump and my face was smashed on the ground in cold, damp leaves that had recently fallen. His strength and size had a major advantage of control over me. Resistance was futile. Forever etched in my memory was his heavy breathing and throbbing grip, which rendered me totally helpless. Suddenly, I heard fizzles in my head and running water, as in a rapid stream. I must have passed out. Then I heard leaves and twigs crunch as the assailant was fleeing away without saying a word.

I tried to get myself together. My mind was saying all kinds of things, like, *What happened? Get up; do something.* But my body would not respond. Slowly, as I heard the trains in the distance, the flow of a stream, and music far off, I came to my senses, realizing I had been raped, sexually assaulted. The dark, wooded area was off Falls Road and next to the Jones Falls water stream, which ran parallel to the railroad tracks at that point. As the club music played loudly in the background, I could not help but imagine that he had taken my car. The bark of the branches had scraped the skin off the shin of both my legs. I brushed the dirt and debris off myself. My tremor of pain and numbness was eclipsed by the awareness that I was very much alive.

Until writing this account, my cousin Billy and the doctors had been the only people who had known what happened years ago. Time truly heals the embarrassment of being totally powerless under someone's control. I felt the anger toward my assailant was brewed within reliving my memory of being helpless and needing to do something to get that back. Now I realize there are many sick people who feel the need to express themselves in vile, hostile, and illicit ways to advance a sense of control for their self-advantage. All ethics aside, if they can get away with something, it provides them a warped sense of satisfaction despite the consequences to others and even to themselves.

My car was still there as I cautiously approached. I was confused and conflicted. *Should I go to the police? Should I go to the hospital?* When I pulled up at the hospital, a policeman was sitting in his car. My mind and emotions could not think of what to say or even the determination to get out of my car to approach him. I drove off and went home to my aunt's. She was away on a cruise, and I am not sure what I would have done if she was home. I soaked a long time in the bathtub, praying. I played gospel music to ease myself to sleep. The next day, I went to work and called my primary doctor, who had me come right in. My doctor was caring and sensitive and made me comfortable enough to reveal the story. I insisted I did not want others to know, and he suggested I seek professional help and counsel.

Time heals and changes occur, for better or worse. I could get help and reach out, even when I did not want to. My ancestors had no choice to reach out openly in a system supportive of slavery. I believe God gave my family ancestors the inspiration to tap into that which the divine has instilled within us. Even as a society over time forced itself upon one race of people, Negroes, blacks, or people of color extorted a sense of privilege and control. God was ever present, imparting His authority in each situation and others.

Often we do not understand even now why or when things happen when they do. My cousin Billy's being there to listen was a godsend that helped unravel the ever-growing snowball effect of feelings or change building within me. I was encouraged and emotionally energized to hold on to God's unchanging hand and divine promise. Now I truthfully know and witness that the battles I face are not mine alone; they are the Lord's also.

I was reluctant to say anything to my buddy Grady about what had happened. I gradually withdrew from visiting him, even though we talked over the phone periodically. The one visit I did make was to see him at the hospice, and I casually mentioned Johnson. In the back of my mind was revenge, but Grady let me know that Johnson had a terrible, untimely death several months earlier. I asked no other questions and changed the subject toward my weak buddy. He wanted a Bible. I went to my car, which still had a visible mark in its steering wheel from the knife. Praiseful, I retrieved the only study Bible I had and gladly gave it to my weary buddy. That was the last time I saw him, even though we had many brief phone calls, which ended with his being extremely tired and most grateful for the Bible. The last time I called, the nurse said he had "peacefully died in his sleep over a week ago," and supposedly no one knew how to contact me for his internment. I asked about his items, and she said his sister only took his Bible. I said, "Good," comforted in knowing Grady was at peace and the Bible was with his family.

I lived in Baltimore City for more than ten years with my aunt Dot. I worked for a family-owned corporation, went to school, and traveled back to Harford County every weekend to attend church. I enjoyed working in the accounting office and with the people who had become family. The company expanded and moved farther from my home when I decided to find a job closer to the home I had purchased in Havre de Grace.

I have come to realize that life is much more complex than what we physically see. What is perceived to be bad for one may only be a challenge that can be overcome. The big picture of it all is that we are who we are with our strengths and weaknesses, which link together to help one another live along supportively. God is with us in all our situations as we live out His purpose for His purpose.

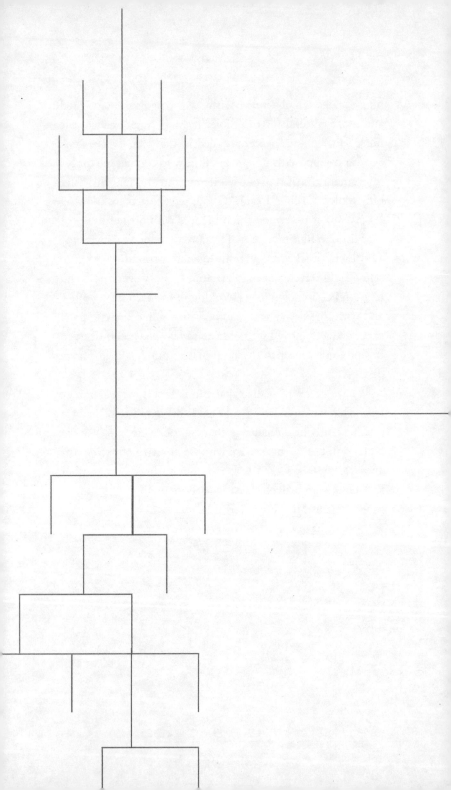

PEOPLE OF COLOR

People of color were adaptable and transformed themselves to deal with conditions and situations engulfing them during many centuries of being overall dominated. For many it was just the way things were to be. A whole race because of the dark color of its skin had been systematically indoctrinated to think that there was no other way to live. Even those assimilated and born as a product of those who controlled and enslaved had no other choice but to follow.

Generations later, the stigma of being the product of a slaveholder is somewhat lightened today by saying, "My family comes from a line with Native American blood." Within the African American community, the shade of our skin varies in many hues and textures. The Bishop-Bond family is no exception, which includes members with skin smooth and jet-black to bright, ruddy, light, and all those in between, like caramel or copper-toned.

Pop Lawson Harris and his mother were labeled mulatto, as were some of John Durbin's children. Whether with voluntary intentions or by infiltration, a race became a mixed people of color. As a product by force of nature within the generational tier, we link to various cultures and races. Family names originate from many different areas of the world and have no direct geographical connection with the family in America. People of color have become African Americans by race, culture, and where we live. Because of what this group had gone through, life reshaped a unique identity. These individuals involuntarily displaced, were stripped of their original identity, which redefined who they were through time and circumstance. Even though they were from various tribes, cultures, and backgrounds, people of color in America are unique from any other race in the world.

My father's grandmother Mom Amelia's father was Lawson Harris; his parents were Hazzard and Amelia "Milly" Harris. Milly was born and raised a slave near Churchville a few miles north of Gravel Hill and west of Darlington. Her freedom certificate describes her as follows:

> Negro Milly
> Maryland Harford County
> I hereby certify that the bearer hereof Negro, a
> bright mulatto woman, thirty-two years of age,
> five feet, five inches high, small scar on the upper
> part of her right breast, square-made and pleasant
> countenance, was raised in Harford County and
> here became free in virtue of a deed of manumis-
> sion executed by Elizabeth Coale on the thirteenth
> day of April in the year eighteen hundred twenty-
> two and recorded among the land record book of
> Harford County Court.
> In testimony whereof, I have hereto set my hand
> and affixed seal of Harford County Court this
> seventeenth day of May, eighteen hundred and
> thirty-two.

Identified by Robert Parker
Henry Dorsey, clerk

In 1899, her death tribute and certificate state she was a reputed 121-old woman. She obviously was not that old. Her children's age and other freedom documents confirm that she was 100 years old at her death. Furthermore, her 1832 freedom paper states she was thirty-two and freed ten years prior by Elizabeth Coale, as recorded in land record HD6 folio25.

> To all who this may concern, be it known that I, Elizabeth Coale, of Harford County and State of Maryland, for divers good causes and Considerations me thereunto moving as also in further consideration of fifty Dollars Current money to me in hand paid have released from Slavery Liberated manumitted and set free and by these presents do manumit liberate and set free my Negro woman named Sarah being forty-one years of age and being able to work and gain a sufficient livelihood and maintenance and the said Negro woman Sarah I do declare to be henceforth free manumitted and discharged from and remain of servitude or service to me my executors or administrators forever and I do also hereby manumit and set free at the time they may arrive at the age of thirty one years the following Children of Sarah aforesaid To wit
>
> Hannah, now ten years of age, Sarah, six years of age, James, five years of age, and Henry, two years of age. All of which children I do declare to be free from all manner of servitude or service after they

may respectively arrives to the age of thirty one years To me my executor or administrators forever and I do further manumit and set free from Slavery my Mulatto woman named Milly aged twenty-two years after she may arrives to the age of thirty-one years also her two children George now five years of age and Eliza now two years of age the same I do also hereby declare to be free and manumitted after they may arrive at the age of thirty one years from all manner of servitude or service to me any executors or administrators forever In Testimony whereof I have hence unto set my hand and affixed my seal this Thirteenth Day of April Eighteen hundred and twenty two.

In presence of Christopher Wilson Elizabeth Cole seal

Thomas Jay

Received on the day of the date of the within mentioned the sum of fifty dollars current money it being the full consideration money within mentioned

Elizabeth Cole seal

Harford County To wit

On the 30th Day of April 1822 personally appeared Elizabeth Coale party to the within Instrument of writing before the subscriber a justice of the peace for said County and acknowledged the same to be her act and deed for the purposes within mentioned and the within mentioned Negroes to be discharged from all servitude or service to her or any claiming render hand to be free and manumitted after they may arrived at the respective ages within mentioned according to the acts of assembly in such cases made and provided acknowledged before me Thomas Jay

Received and recorded the second Day of May, eighteen hundred & twenty-two & examined by Henry Dorsey, clk

This document helped me link other family members also listed, even though Milly's relationship to the older woman and her children was not specified. Pop Lawson's death certificate and three of his siblings confirm Mom Milly's maiden name as Prigg. My journey linking my family history continues with another family connection.

In the early 1800s, the Prigg family name was common through the Darlington/Dublin portion of Harford County and into Cecil County. Many of these families owned slaves and had huge farms. Although most documents concerning slaves do not list a last name, I could piece families as a group by their names and ages together compared against other listings and documents. I was able to locate the Priggs by last name in the 1832 free sheriff's listing and compare the families listed near them for possible relatives to match up in my research. I matched my names from the 1822 manumission of Sarah and Hanna. James and Henry were listed next to Mark Prigg, age fifty. My family was gradually being revealed and coming together as I searched for more documents to confirm their links, adding even more family history.

I discovered many interesting court cases relating to the validation of the freedom of people of color. I can imagine many free people were concerned about being kidnapped and sold south into slavery. I suppose runaways, accusations, and misapprehensions occurred frequently. Free people of color, without proper documentation, were always at risk of being falsely captured and sold as slaves farther south. A good, trusted white friend and clear freedom papers would be particularly crucial to secure protection to work. I believe the community depended on one another throughout this part of the county—those free and enslaved. I had come across many references to a young apprentice wanting to learn a trade and skill and indentured for a period of time. Many friends not believing in the sanction of slavery supported the maintenance and sustenance of free people of color by providing work. Work not readily available to them, I could see them banding together to support one another.

On August 20, 1832, a petition was filed in the county court to secure validation of Sarah Prigg and her children. Albert Constable files for the petitioners Mark and Sarah Prigg, his wife, which state:

> To the Hon'b the Judge of Harford County Court
> The Petitioner of Mark Prigg & Sarah, his wife (Negro) of Harford County humbly show unto your honor that a certain *Charles Gilbert* late of the same county and who departed this life about the year 1797 did a short time previous to his decease given to his stepdaughter *Elizabeth Coale* your petitioner Sarah and that the said *Elizabeth* immediately took said Sarah unto her possession and continued to hold her up to the period of her manumission.— That four years afterwards your petitioner Sarah

was seized for a debt due to some person from a certain *Skipworth Coale* (who was then the husband of said *Elizabeth Coale*) and exposed to public sale and at which sale a certain *Thomas Hall* became the purchaser for the use and benefit of said *Elizabeth Coale* and after said sale made or present of your petitioner Sarah to said *Elizabeth Coale* for her sole and separate use.

And your petitioner further shows that the said *Elizabeth Coale* took immediate possession of your Petitioner Sarah & held her to her sole and separate use until *30th April 1822*, when she manumitted your petitioner, Sarah, which was regularly acknowledged and recorded agreeable to law will more fully appear by reference to a certified copy hereof hencewith presented—

Yours petitioner further shows that for many years prior to this term last aforesaid they lived together and been recognized as man and wife and had a number of children among which are the following to Wit: Hannah, Sarah, James & Henry and that afterward to wit on the *27th day April 1824* the said *Elizabeth Coale* did bargain & sell for a valuable consideration unto your petitioner Mark his aforesaid children Hannah, Sarah, James & Henry and did deliver this same unto the possession of your Petitioner Mark and also execute and deli'd unto your petitioner Mark a valid bill of sale thereof or will more fully appear by a reference to the same which he herewith presence.

That afterward your petitioner had issued another daughter called Pricilla and that since then the said Hannah (one of the aforesaid children of your petitioners) has had issue a son called Harrison and that all the said children as well as said grandchild have ever since thence aforesaid manumission been

and still are in the actual possession of your petitioners and all of whom are minors under the age
of twenty-one years. And your petitioners further
shows that some evil disposed persons pretending
to doubt the freedom of the aforesaid children of
your petitioners or the right and legal title of your
petitioners to them have made divers secrets and
clandestine efforts to rob your petitioners of said
children by forcible means and without resorting to
the process of the Law—wherefore your petitioners
have deemed it their duty to make this statement of
the title by which they claim their said children and
pray your Honors to secure order in the premises
declaring your petitioner Sarah to be free and their
said children to be the property of your Petitioner
Mark, who owns himself to have been at the time of
said purchase and title to be a free coloured inhabit-
ant of Harford County in the State of Maryland
Albert Constable
for petitioners
Maryland Harford County
to Wit on this 20th day of
August in the year 1832 personally appeared before
me a Justice of Peace for the State & County aforesaid Mark Prigg(free Negro) of said State & County
and made oath on the Holy Evangelist of Almighty
God, that all and singular the matters and things
stated in the aforesaid Petition are true— Sworn
before, John Hopkins

Maryland Harford County
to Wit on this 20th day
of August eighteen hundred and thirty-two personally appeared before me a Justice of Peace for state
and County aforesaid Christopher Wilson of state

& county aforesaid and did affirms and saith that he intermarried with the Daughter of Skipworth Coale who is mentioned in the a foregoing petition and believes the matters and thereof the now stated to be true & further saith that he was present at the said sale of said Negro Sarah mentioned in said petition and he and the said Thomas Hall purchased in the said Sarah in the sole and separate use of said Elizabeth Coale and immediately thence after hand this said Thomas Hall give the said Sarah to said Elizabeth Coale

Sworn before
affirmed to before Jos. Worthingtion
Filed August 21st, 1832

My foreparents, by whatever means necessary, filed for the liberating security of their family. It let me know they pursued against all odds to move on from others' total control. The act of passing a person to another person as property without regards to family consideration was grossly insensible. My mind's eye gives me the sense to think Elizabeth Coale did what she did out of affection for a family she had known all her life. I can imagine the explosive emotions in the forcible separation due to the collecting on her husband's financial debts. A God-created person cannot compare in worth to a home sold at public sale to collect on debt. We have a single attachment to a material house, but we have many emotional bonds to the spirit of a person, especially a loved one who had become a member of a close-knit family.

I see a truly honest man in Pop Mark Prigg. He continued to pull his family together, out from the dividing grips of slavery. In 1836, he purchased thirty-four-year-old Fanny from Elizabeth Coale and two children separated by obligated financial transactions. Pop Mark worked tirelessly for the security of his family. At the age of fifty-eight, he purchased from Elisha Greenland for twenty-five dollars children Milly, age three, and one-year-old Sylvester. In the 1840 federal census, Mark Prigg, "head of family," lived in Dist5, Darlington, with twelve other free people of color. This census only names the head of family and has many columns to be checked or numbered with further information.

Free Colored Persons – Males—
Under 10: 4
Free Colored Persons – Males—
10 thru 23: 2
Free Colored Persons – Males—
55 thru 99: 1
Free Colored Persons – Females—
Under 10: 1
Free Colored Persons – Females—
10 thru 23: 1
Free Colored Persons – Females—
24 thru 35: 3
Free Colored Persons – Females—
55 thru 99: 1
Total–All Persons
(Free White, Free Colored, Slaves):13
Persons Employed in Agriculture: 2
Persons Employed in
Manufacture and Trade: 1
Total Free Colored Persons: 13

The 1840 census was the last to use columns and not list the names of those people living within the same household. I presume that Pop Mark and Mom Sarah were the one male and female columned aged fifty-five through ninety-nine years of age. In the petition, the couple stated they had lived as husband and wife long before the term. This statement makes it more than likely they had been together before the death of Charles Gilbert in 1797. It's highly possible Mom Milly, born about 1799, and Fanny, born about 1802, purchased by Mark Prigg, are sisters with other unknown siblings. The description of Mom Milly's complexion was the same as described in Mark Prigg's freedom paper; also the family was listed together in the1832 sheriff's list of free persons.

Negro Mark

Maryland Harford County Court

I hereby certify that the bearer
Here of Negro Mark about fifty-five years of age
five feet five inches and three quarters high
of light complexion and has a scar on
the right of the front part of the right leg
said to have been cut by a sickle said Negro
Mark became free by virtue of a deed of
Manumission executed by Edward Prigg
bearing date the 4th day of February 1822
and recorded in Liber HD no.6 folio21 one of
the Land Record Books of Harford County Court
In testimony thereof
I hereto set my hand and affix the

seal of Harford County Court this
fourth day of November 1833.

Identified by Joseph Prigg
Henry Dorsey, clerk

Pop Mark Prigg, mulatto, purchased himself from slavery
from Edward Prigg along with relatives Daniel and Hugh
Prigg, age forty-three years old. In 1822, Pop Mark, age
thirty-nine, paid seven shillings and six pence for his freedom, as did his two relatives, who also acquired the surname
Prigg. As I observed various Prigg families, most of them
lived for generations in the Darlington area except for the
blacksmith Daniel, who moved southwest, less than twenty
miles to Abingdon.

In the 1820 census, a column asks the number of persons
engaged in agriculture, commerce, and manufacturing. Pop
Mark Prigg had a one in commerce and was listed with one
female, twenty-six to forty-five, two males, and two females
less than fourteen years of age, which confirms his wife,
Sarah, and four children in the petition. He must have had
his own store and trade as merchant. Even though he was
listed as a free person, his Certificate of Freedom stated he
was freed on February 4, 1822. Living with them during the
1840s and engaged in agriculture was Sarah's first daughter, Amelia, with husband, Hazzard Harris, and daughter
Hannah with husband Sam Gordon. Pop Mark Prigg died
before the 1850 census.

Covert Connections

There were many people like Pop Mark Prigg who were smart enough to secure and sustain their liberty and zest for freedom. He lived his life in a community highly concerned for the well-being and nurture of family. The community flourished on a kind sense of inclusion and respect for differences in people. In 1776, the Religious Society of Friends, known as Quakers, banned members who owned slaves. The village of Darlington held true to this conviction in its modest inclusion of free people of color in maintaining a livelihood with education training and integrated land ownership. This Quaker community maintained support for the free people of color and assistance to those enslaved. I believe the Quakers of Darlington were the center of activities in Harford County to promote the abolition of slavery, especially in advancing neighboring free people of color.

Abolitionists in the areas surrounding my family seem to help in many ways to help those enslaved. Some purchased and then set free slaves, some took indentureds to provide a means of providing for family, and many even assisted in aiding fugitives traveling north into Free States.

Historical Sketches of Harford County, Maryland, by Samuel Mason Jr., published known activities within the Darlington community. One account of runaway slaves was confirmation of my feelings of the Bishop-Bond family connection in place along a route lit by the North Star. Land owners established with close family were interwoven throughout time, towns, and talents in working skills linking trails directly to freedom. My family worked together within the community of the covert abolitionists who assisted those escaping slavery. Despite possible deadly consequences of being caught helping escaping slaves, many observers speak of the success along this branch of the Underground Railroad. According to Chris Weeks' extraordinary work, *An Architectural History of Harford County, Maryland*, the county can boast thoroughly documented accounts of Underground Railroad conductor William "Billy" Worthington. His ancestors had been landowners in the area since the early eighteenth century.

> Historian Samuel Mason, whose "own grandfather was twice arrested for helping slaves," wrote in our part of Harford County one of the routes across the river was at Worthington's landing to freedom…in the evening, frequently one of his men would come to him and whisper, "Uncle Billy, there's people on the hill." Then Uncle Billy would order a sheep killed and cooked for the escaping slaves then hiding in the cornfields. After dark, a boat would be available at the landing to take them across the river. Had Harris undertook this service.

My Pop Hazzard Harris certainly provided this service to freedom across the Susquehanna River and up to the river north a few miles to Pennsylvania. Conveniently across the Susquehanna River lived other relatives—among them a son, George Harris. I can picture the tedious route to freedom unfold from the Deep South along merchant paths to Baltimore and following main tracks into waterways of Havre de Grace. As the fugitives dealt with elements of nature and the emotional fear of being pursued by slave catchers, the physical and mental stress totally overwhelmed them every now and then. I can imagine their emotions being overwhelmed at times with thoughts of giving up, turning back, and of wondering where they were.

I am convinced that, despite the danger of being captured, the fugitives from slavery were among more secret undercover friends than enemies when they reached conduits of the Bush River near Abingdon of Harford County. It was an area highly populated with people of color and a station of kindness toward helping their race, including fugitives escaping the harsh South. For those escaping slavery in the Deep South, freedom may have seemed foreign to them, but I can imagine the emotions of reaching a safe haven or hearing someone say "You free now." I see eyes gleam with excitement and a spark of relief in their spirit while traveling under the clear, dark cover of the night, following the direction of the brightest star of hope. With great optimism and spirit, Pop Hazzard Harris rowed these survivors directly to safety beyond the Mason-Dixon Line boundary between a Southern and a free state. The fugitives embarked on a life independent of slavery.

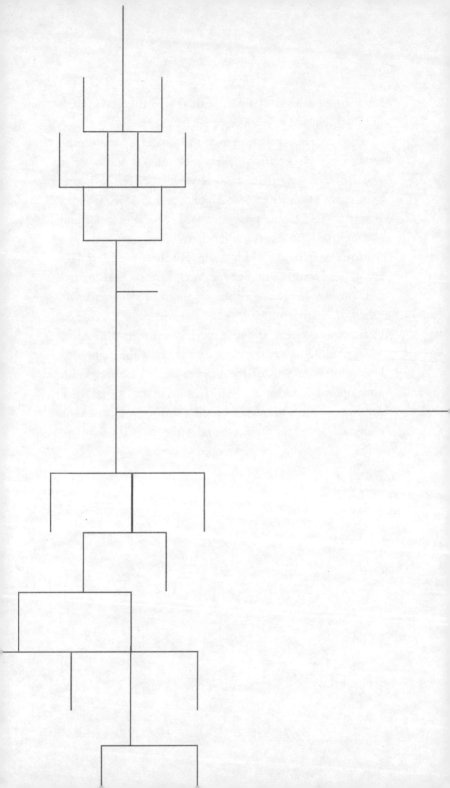

INDEPENDENCE

A Conflicted Hustle

For centuries, most people of color in the United States relied totally on those who had control over them. In extreme cases, they were physically shackled and chained, only seeing the light of day to work a harsh labor for another's benefit. The indignity of being stripped of all control of one's well-being broke the human spirit in a regal race of unique people. Slavery devastated a race, and time transformed them. Negroes from the many tribes survived by holding on to the irrepressible spirit God instilled within. This peculiar race, people of color, endured with a redefined self to become viable citizens of the nation as one tribe, an African American community and family.

The 1832 sheriff's list of free blacks in Harford County lists more than sixteen-hundred people, which includes many of my liberated Bishop-Bond family: Moses, age forty, and wife Fanny Martin, age forty, with five children. John Durbin Gilbert, seventy-two years old, and wife Jane, with several of their children, in-laws, and grandchildren listed. Also was Russell Hill, forty years old, with wife Ruth, who appeared within these same neighbors.

My father's grandmother's grandparents exuded the independence of free people of color in the lands they purchased and organizations established around them. Pop Russell Hill, with wife Ruth, donated land to establish a church within their community family of Gravel Hill. Ironically, John Griffith freed Russell Hill in 1831 and then gave him property and land as payment. I believe he was indentured to work for the land, and the freedom paper was legal protocol to travel. The legal deed to Russell Hill to the land of nine-and-a-half acres in "Gravelly Hills" was recorded on the February 24, 1842, land record HD 26folio151.

Maryland Harford County
I hereby certify that the bearer hereof,
Negro Russell Hill, a black man aged thirty-six
years, five feet, six inches high, has a scar on the
back of the right hand occasioned by a burn, lisps
in his voice and very thick-made, became free in
virtue of a deed of manumission duly executed by
John Griffith and recorded the first day of February
Eighteen hundred and thirty-one among the land
record books of Harford County Court.
In testimony whereof I have hereto
subscribed my name and affixed
the seal of Harford County Court this
first day of February, eighteen hundred
and thirty-one.
Identified by "Isaac Hoopman" Henry Dorsey clerk

I often wondered how the village of Gravel Hill got its name. Was it because of the people of color named "Hill"? The only road through the village that bears its name was made public as recent as the 1940s, when electricity had been installed. Even then areas throughout the community were mined for its resourceful rock into craters of gravel pits. The name is literal for hills full of, or covered with, rock fragments or pebbles. I discovered the earliest notation of its title in the 1783 tax assessments record, which called it "Gravelly Hills." Even with its harsh, rasping name, I think of pleasant, billowing slopes and a streamed valley that create the natural springs of refreshing water, sustaining the life of generations and the Bishop-Bond family.

The Hill family owned land all throughout the Gravel Hill and Chapel Road areas, which are connected by a road leading to Lapidum. Family members mention that before the construction of I-95 in the 1960s, family frequently walked to other family homes, which are now divided by this busy highway. Another family cemetery is near there with several Hill and Johnson names on tombstones.

In the 1832 sheriff's list, Pop Russell Hill was listed directly under Toney Hill, age seventy years old. I presume Toney to be Russell's father. As I browse for information in the few records available for people of color, I realize it's a rarity. The fact was that laws during this time rarely allowed individuality of people of color. It was not considered normal by the pro-slavery majority who were privy to legal advantages over people of color even beyond enslavement.

In the census records, which only list the head of household before 1840, Pop Russell Hill was listed with eight other free persons. Also listed were Gerrard, John, Milkey, and Abraham Hill, all free in districts two and five. I presume they were relatives. Pop Toney Hill was listed in the 1830 record next to Gerrard. In the 1820 census, Tower Hill was listed with eight free people. I believe Toney and Tower was the same person, as no other information for free people of color were stated on this census. There was another Negro Tower listed at over forty-five with a free female.

Like Pop Mark Prigg in 1820, Tower Hill lived in the Darlington area with one female over forty-five, one male between fourteen and twenty-six, one male less than fourteen, and two females less than fourteen. The move to make a decent living in the area between Darlington and Havre de Grace was common for free people of color. Pop Harry, Moses, and Priscilla Bond, aged between fourteen and twenty-six, are listed alone in the second district around Gravel Hill near Pop John Durbin in the 1820 census.

Tower Hill was listed with ten free persons in the 1810 census and three free persons in the first US census of 1790. The 1800 census does not list free people of color. Tower Hill purchased his wife, Elizabeth, and daughter from Edward C. Tolley and set them free in 1800. In 1804 and 1806, court records stated Tower Hill and sons cleared and worked on a certain man's land; the man refused to pay them, and the justice of the peace ruled against him. After the judgment, this man destroyed property with his horse-driven wagon and assaulted Tower Hill.

The 1790 census notes Tower Hill with two other Negros with the name Tower. Hill was the only surname given. In 1783, federal tax assessments listed Tower manumitted by James Rigbie in Deer Creek, which is along the Susquehanna River in Harford County.

Negro Tower
State of Maryland, Harford County, to wit

I hereby certify that the bearer hereof,
Negro Tower, five feet, nine inches high, of a black
complexion, about fifty years of age, became free on
the fifteenth day of September, seventeen hundred
and eighty-one by virtue of a deed of Manumission
made by James Rigbie and Nathan Rigbie of said
county and duly executed and recorded. The said
Negro Tower was raised in the county aforesaid
and has a scar below the left eye and another
on the left leg.
Identified by
John Williams
as testifyth freed
In testimony whereof, I have here unto set my
hand and affixed the seal of my office this fourth
day of July in
the year eighteen hundred and seven
Henry Dorsey, clk

In 1775, the American Revolution against the British began. Even though slavery in America existed since 1619, America's fight for freedom became a platform to escape slavery. Slaves biding for freedom fought on both sides, given a promise of being set free. The new day that the black soldiers had fought so hard to attain was never realized. It did, however, lead some whites to question the institution of slavery. These whites came to see the contradictions in thought as they applied to the rights of the black man. Unfortunately, these whites were far outnumbered by the whites who were blind to the inconsistencies in American ideologies and slavery. This white majority could justify these contradictions by maintaining that blacks were not a part of the sociopolitical community and, therefore, had no right to enjoy the freedom and equality gained in the war.

However, upon his service in the American Revolution, Tower, aged about twenty-four in 1781, had returned home from his battalion, discharged for having a wife and children to support and take care of. He was set free afterward by the Rigbie brothers of Darlington. I found Tower's name in a history book on a list of soldiers discharged to return home. He was not actually certified free until July 4, 1807, well after the end of the war.

Their continued quest for freedom led to more white and black contact. Even though the war failed to emancipate them, they began to experience a sense of distinct identity. This identity reflected the essential values of the War for Independence. The identity flourished into a collective sense of community. The establishment of local black churches before and after the war played an integral role in creating the sense of community, like the African Methodist Episcopal Church founded by Richard Allen. Through the churches, the free African Americans came to the understanding that they were the ones who best upheld the "revolutionary tradition" of social justice, equality, and, most of all, freedom.

The Revolution gave people of color a chance to assert their drive for freedom. While the Revolution did not emancipate them, it unified their belief of freedom. It aided in the creation of a sense of community and gave them a platform from which to fight for the eventual eradication of slavery. Whether Tower had served voluntarily or not, he had an opportunity beyond the confines of a plantation to explore. I can imagine stories of his journey as he returned home to support his family, linking legacy unto generations even unto the Bishop-Bond family.

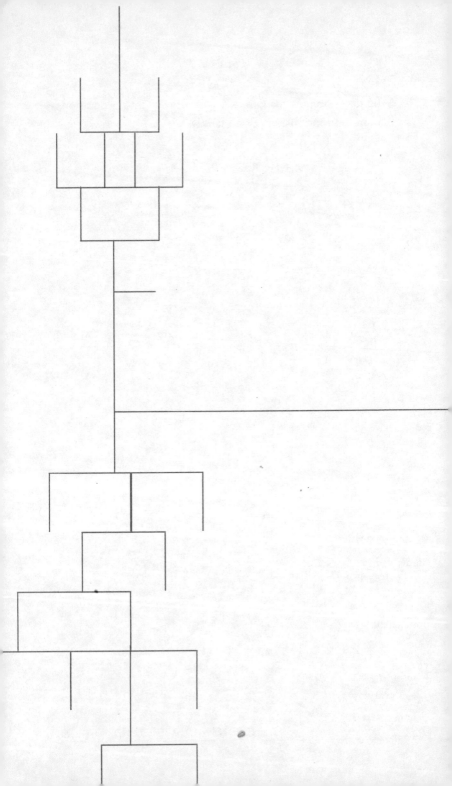

CONCLUSION

"My name is Geraldine Bishop-Hague, and I am the matriarch of the Bishop, Bond families and St. James AME Church. I have been a member of the church for over eighty years, where I have witnessed my nephew, Reggie, grow through the many challenges of juvenile diabetes. God has blessed him to have come out as 'pure gold.'

"I saw my nephew first as a toddler hiding from me, clinging to the legs of his mother. After moments of careful observation and a wide smile ear-to-ear, he approached me with a big hug. He has always been close to assist me with food and information for family gatherings. It does not surprise me of his deeply inspiring writing about the family. I am extremely proud of Reggie and all the hard work in tracing the family history. "

—Aunt Dot

This is a tribute I write to my loving nephew, Reginald Bishop. For he has shown great endurance to gain the knowledge needed to complete a task many have started and few have finished. Thank you, Reggie, for caring so much about your lineage; you wrote a book about and for all of your family. Future generations will marvel at knowing about us who have gone before. I thank you on behalf of my children and their children not yet born.

—Uncle Albert

My quest to confirm questionable family stories I heard as a child from the Bishop-Bond family has resulted in an incredible journey. I have shared myself and my discoveries in the treasure trove of history revealed. The conclusion to this book is only the beginning of your journey in tracing your family history. When I started researching, I had much to learn, but through patience and persistence, my endeavor became a rewarding historical lesson in life and personal experience. We are who we are as links of one another, genetically and through generational experience.

Many African Americans assume they are unable to trace their family roots before the Civil War. In many cases, it is possible to discover a heritage of rich family information. You can, as I did, preserve a written history for present and future generations. I hope I have helped inspire, motivate, and encourage those who would take the journey to compile their family roots in history.

People of color through the ages have made major contributions to our country and world. These unsung heroes and heroines are the threads interwoven within the fabric and foundation of our country. They are who made Americans who we are today. I offer tribute to those known and unknown influential parts of who I have become in life.

I salute all people of color with the entwined links of my family whose full story is yet to be discovered through my research. I believe people who plant a seed will always leave behind a legacy, by genetics, by deed, or by what they have done in maintaining their livelihood. Within our family are hidden trails in time for generations to trace back, uncovering an unknown destination unto our roots with family history. I have planted much love, time, effort, and resources as a devotion to reveal my family's history. I uncovered myself through the process and hope this may be my legacy for others to research.

The Bishop-Bond, Finding Yourself through Your Family Roots has revealed people of color born in the mid-1700s before the birth of the United States of America. Once a slave, Tower Hill was liberated, set free, and released from servitude, he maintained a livelihood for himself, his community, and his family.

Sarah was enslaved to Elizabeth Coale, set free with children in 1822, proved by way of a legalized petition in 1832. She married Mark Prigg and had several children while enslaved, ultimately purchasing each of their freedom together. Their oldest daughter, Amelia, married Hazzard Harris and continued the family's devoted pursuit to advance people of color with major roles in successfully assisting efforts on the Underground Railroad.

Mark Prigg, enslaved unto Edward Prigg, was released and set free in February 1822 at age thirty-nine after paying seven shillings and six pence. At the same time, Daniel and Hugh Prigg also paid the identical amounts to purchase their own freedom. Together they helped strengthen, support, and build the growing community of free people of color.

Encouraged with the progress, cousins Cupid Peaker, Moses Harris, Pop William Bond, Pop John Gilbert Durbin, Pop Moses Martin, and others purchased land, laying foundations for African American communities. Free people of color owned land, cultivated family, and developed a close sense of community during hostile times from the War of Independence to the Civil War between the States.

A family legacy within the communities of Harford County continued with the establishment of religious, educational, and social institutions. The African American soldiers returning home with renewed hope and inspiration for their homes helped build churches on lands donated by their fore-parents, like Pop Russell and Mom Ruth Hill. These parents, as others, provided a secure, stable home for generations, which had become the home place. Within the safe haven village of Gravel Hill, families grew, learned, and worshiped with unity that outreached to several others.

Despite moving away from the county, my father's grandparents, Pop Augustus with Mom Celesta Bishop and Pop George and Mom Amelia Bond, returned to support a growing community. Great-aunts and great-uncles provided a nurturing structure by being integral pillars of strength, wisdom, and kindness in their homes, church, and public. My grandparents Pop Oscar and Mom Sarah Bishop had done the best they could with a large growing family that projected much affection. They were being the complemented union to produce the Bishop-Bond family of connections.

We are who we are as links of one another. I link with many cousins and various people like my father. Despite our differences, my father, George Bishop, and I link with others in the same way. This connection with him, an athletic coach throughout the community and I an intellectual mentor throughout the country, was part of his lineage to me.

We both could relate to all people of different ages from many backgrounds and various aspects in life.

My family history reveals who I am as links of my ancestors. I have discovered, through tracing my roots, a family firmly grounded by a divine foundation. The research and documentation revealed people with a resilience to adapt to adverse situations. Beyond the challenges of everyday circumstances, an inner strength persists within my family, linking unique bonds throughout the villages and the community. Despite unique problems and struggles to trace my roots with documentation, the overall sense of appreciation has been revealed to me through the lives and times within family history. Finally, at the end of the day, family is all we have—an everlasting bond and eternal kinship.

The Bishop-Bond family, as I see it, has interwoven ties within us all. Through my eyes, our people of color's deep, secured family roots have been a pillar of strength, a beacon of hope, and an extremely rich bond from end to end, linking past generations to future generations.

Step-by-Step Lessons Learned

Your Life's Story

Our experiences throughout life provide us with lessons. I often say as we face each day, acknowledge and learn something from every day. In each day's lesson is a message, an example of life's rewards or warnings. Through my involvement in tracing my family tree, I have learned step-by-step the overall knowledge learned during the process is great. Finding a single piece, a nugget of personal family history, is a treasure more than compensating for the overwhelming disappointments in not finding any information at all.

For all beginners in family history, learning lessons in patience and persistence is crucial. Locating family documents is time consuming. The key to the quest is to get started documenting what you know by mapping out your family search. With focused persistence in the historical pursuit, the rewards of a full tree with amazing story lessons can be accomplished. My experience is proof to inspire and encourage all persons to start tracing and compiling their family roots.

Family history, starts with you, whether a researcher or not. You can trace the descent of your family to build on the lines within your pedigree. Knowing and listing records of your line of ancestry enhances the validity to who you are generations to come.

Begin writing your life story, remembering the oral family stories and elders as far back as you can recall. Pull those clues in old diaries and letters to trigger your memories to leads of researching into your ancestors. Once you have explored the depths of past memories, the real search begins. Pulling out the crucial information to assist in your journey is the trails of clues and signs to direct you. Gathering and investigating specific names, places, and times are the major elements in family research. I have found having more oral information of my father's line prompted me to focus my research on my mother's line initially. In any investigation, the quest to answer a certain question usually is the goal and focus. The question of how the Bishop and Bond family connected to a modest community along the Susquehanna River in Maryland was in my mind. Furthermore, the statement from my grandfather of my being related to all of Harford County was a driving force in retrieving undiscovered family history.

Writing personal history is a very thought-provoking process. Taking time out to revisit old photos, scrapbooks, and things with sentimental value brings about memories to write about. Extremely helpful is detailed information in personal diaries, journals, and family Bibles. Tracing family roots involves extracting family names, places, and times from resources of all kinds. It is very important to organize, note the resources, and keep a log of from whom and where you retrieved the information. I have found over time this to be extremely helpful, especially the larger your family tree grows and the more documented information you accumulate. Over the years of backtracking and researching, I have learned to log my research days.

Interviews

Your own personal story, like my life's journal, raised questions that to triggered the thoughts of older relatives I needed to talk to. You will get good information by offering to write a relative's biography or life's story, no matter their age. Requesting them to write their own and to give you a copy also works. Instead of a formal interview to get family information, a few family questions over time and visits seemed to be my best approach. Indeed this done strategically is more rewarding with older members who think of the questions between visits instead of bombarding them with many family questions. To my surprise, it has become easier to ask about family than retrieving old photos and family documents to copy, which have deep sentimental values. Interviewing a close family friend or longtime neighbor can be helpful in acquiring photos, obituaries, and histories, which include family members.

In researching family history and tracing roots, it helps to focus on one or two lines in a certain period of time. I may search for a line on my father's side for a month and on my mother's line another, even though while investigating, certain family names often show up with connections to switch your research direction. Log your days, take notes, and stay organized with family files. Now you have recalled and recorded the earliest family memories. You have interviewed and retrieved information from family and friends. The journey has begun to trace your family roots and history. There are many readings available and workshops on tracing family roots to further advance family research.

On the Vital Hunt

By using the specific information retrieved from your family stories and information, finding records to verify and confirm the data is sought after. Every seventy-two years after taking the Federal Census, schedules are made available to the public. The 1940 census is the latest attainable. These records taken every ten years since 1790 are ideal to find your ancestors for information to confirm with additional documentation. Each column within the schedules offers vital information, which aid in compiling family history. Note indexes should only be used to find the original copy, which oftentimes has misspellings or discrepancies. The 1890 census in most states were destroyed by fire; other documents, like city directories, can be used.

Many times the census information leads to other vital records and vice versa. Vital or primary records are facts of an individual from that person and generated nearest to the event of their birth, marriage, or death. In many cases, especially African American genealogy, oral stories and information in a Bible may be all there is connecting early family. The quest in tracing family history is confirming family connections with various resources from the information compiled. Birth certificates are released one hundred years after issued in most states unless legally obtained by judgment. Old marriage certificates can be given upon request at the local historical society. The license application, which may give parents' names, can be viewed at the courthouse and state archives. Social Security applications can be purchased after finding information on the relative in the Social Security death index. Death certificates in many states began in the late 1800s and are indexed at the state archives. Many of these records can be ordered online, by phone, or by letter.

Vital records are the base in tracing your roots through the twentieth century. The research can be challenging when you are unable to locate actual documents. The records could be in different forms and in many places. For example, fraternities, hospitals, and churches, to name a few, may no longer have records, or they may be kept in archives. When your family research is at a roadblock, the state and national archives is the place to be for vital information.

Leads to Data

African American history has unique difficulties, especially before 1870. Those of us on this quest to trace our family roots necessarily get creative at this point of researching. Certainly, additional factors are taken into consideration, like history, region, laws, status, and others. African Americans have been faced with generations of challenges and, nevertheless, prevail. When it comes to the law and doing things, each locality handled records differently always to the advantage of whites. Nationally, blacks were treated as property and third-class citizens up to the time the civil rights laws took place in the 1960s, about one hundred years after slavery.

Finding relatives before the Civil War becomes even more problematic. Knowledge of some history can play into tracking down crucial information to locate connections to family. For instance, I only knew the last name of a several-great-grandfather. In looking for more data to add to my family's history, I came across a census schedule of veterans in 1890. After browsing through the entire document line by line, I took note of those men with possible family last names. The bottom of the listing gave the post office in which they resided near. With a last name that matched my relative, I could note his military unit and request the pension records from the national archives. Upon receiving the full file, I could read of his military service and the fact that he was shot in the right arm. I read his physical description, names of childhood friends, the area he grew up in, marriage date with witnesses' names, wife's complete name and birthday, their two children's names and birthdates, and the date he died. With his death date, I could order the certificate that listed his parents and cemetery he is buried in. Upon finding this treasure trove of information, I connected my family roots to trace even more branches in my tree.

When relatives are not listed in the 1860 free census schedules, the question considered by the researcher should be whether or not they were free or enslaved. The free African Americans listed in the 1860 census most likely carried papers, which had been registered at the local county courthouse. These Certificates of Freedom and or manumission papers listed their name, full physical description, age, name of the person who set him or her free, and the date. Land records of the free persons could list information, especially after the Civil War, when a large quantity of blacks purchased land.

When relatives were enslaved, they had no more than a monetary value to many who kept them. In many documents, African Americans are referred to as "property" or "slave of ...," "Negro of ...," or mentioned by first name only. Slaves in the 1850 and 1860 slave schedules are listed without names under the slave owners' name by ages. Several slave owners were compensated for enlisting and setting free black men to serve the military in the war. Most transactions exchanging goods for slaves were documented but do not always list the slave's name. The historical society archives many copies of these transactions, including bill of sales, etc.

If your relative is listed in the 1870 census and not in the 1860 census, you can consider that they were slaves. This is where research gets unique. Explore the community, browse through all the neighbors, and take note of those nearby in the 1870 and 1880 census. The majority of those freed by the Emancipation Proclamation reluctantly moved far away. Many stayed on or near the land of their previous slave owners. Observe those large-valued estates near the relative in the 1870 census and check his location and name in the 1860 slave schedule. Under his name, compare the group of slaves by age. If the group is fairly close, more than likely that is your relative's family. With the slave owner's name, you can search court records, land records, newspapers, and family archive books and papers for the mentioning of information on his slaves.

Tracing family history before the war involves investigating certain co-relationships of neighbors and slave owners. Most slaves will be listed under the transaction of their owner and may be listed in probate court, chattel records, and wills. I discovered an 1831 court paper that lists slaves with ages who traveled with their owners from Pittsylvania County, Virginia, to Harford County, Maryland. A law required the slave owners moving from another state with slaves to file with the county. I traced my several-great-grandmother to this document by way of other legal transactions. According to the trail of court records and transactions, the person who set her free attained her in lieu of debt owed by the family from Virginia. The paper states she was part of the dowry to the Virginia wife. Some slaves have unique first names that can be matched easily to documents. Many slaves will never be documented because of a lack of legal activity of the slave owner.

On the other hand, many of those free people of color before the war were required to register their status or prove it by a recorded white witness. Each Certificate of Freedom and manumission noted one or two witnesses when a person of color had been freed. In 1832, the sheriff for the county was required by the state to list all free people of color by household, name, and age. This listing of about 1,600 free blacks in Harford County has become a great resource for my research tracing my family roots. My family history uniquely links many branches of my family tree to several free people of color listed. It allowed me to follow up in land as well as court records, filling my family's history with more data.

African American research can be challenging. Be persistent in learning where documents are, and you will prevail. As you research family roots, learn step-by-step the process of recovering a heritage revealed in many branches of an extraordinary family tree and history. The quest begins with you and your family stories. Discover a remarkable journey tracing your family roots.

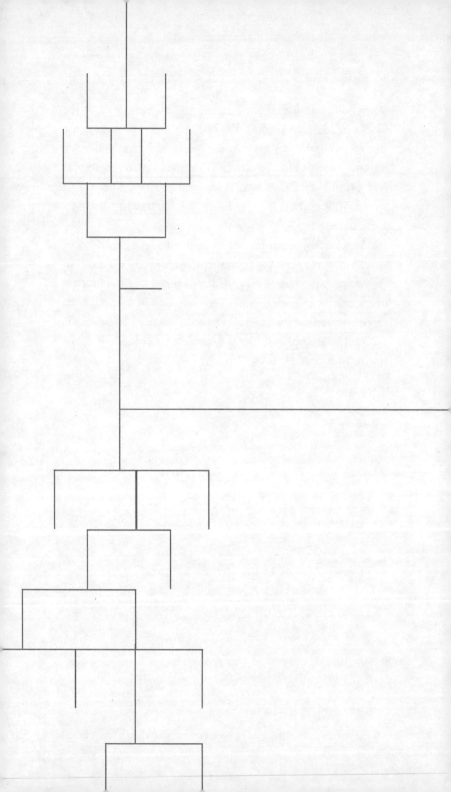

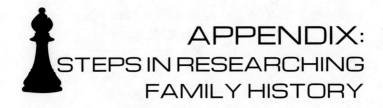

APPENDIX: STEPS IN RESEARCHING FAMILY HISTORY

1. *Oral Stories* – Family Documents/Collections

    1. Focus on the details—names, places, and time periods.

2. *US Census* – Taken every ten years since 1790, family details since 1850.

    1. Released for public access after seventy-two (72) years.

3. *Marriage License and Certificates*

    1. Focus on details of license, person issued to, certificate lists age and place.

    2. County courthouse present records back to 1860s with details.

4. *Land Records* – County records since 1700s to present

    1. Often gives relationships like wife, parents, siblings, neighbors, etc.

5. *Social Security Application/Benefits* – Since 1937

   1. Application signed by actual person, lists parents and place of birth.

6. *Death Certificate/Obituary* – Since 1898

   1. Parents, place of birth, spouse, and possible other relationships.

7. *Register of Wills* – Since the 1800s

   1. Relationships of parents, children, etc.

8. *Court Records* – Civil/Criminal cases

9. *Veteran Records* – Enlistment/Draft rolls list age, birth place

   1. Military pension records.

10. *Freedom Papers* –From 1700s through 1866

    1. Certificate of Freedom—age, description of freeperson, ref proof.

    2. Manumission—lists slaveholder, name, age, and date freed.

    3. 1832 Freed Negro Census—full name, age listed by household.

    4. Freedom via wills, land records, etc.

11. *Miscellaneous Documents* – Freedman Bank Records; newspaper slave purchase documents

Chart no. _____ on chart no. _____
No. 1 on this chart is the same as no. _____ on chart no. _____

1 George Wesley Bishop
b: Apr. 9, 1940
p: Havre de Grace, MD
m: Aug. 3, 1964
d: Oct. 3, 1995
p: Havre de Grace, MD
sp: **Anne Lee Lewis**

2 Oscar Jerome Bishop
b: Mar. 31, 1899
p: Havre de Grace, MD
m: Mar. 30, 1922
d: Aug. 1, 1979
p: St. James Gravel Hill

3 Sarah Amelia Bond
b: Nov. 28, 1902
p: Havre de Grace, MD
d: Jan. 14, 1966
p: St. James Gravel Hill

4 Augustus Bishop
b: Nov. 29, 1874
p: Havre de Grace, MD
m: Dec. 14, 1898
d: abt 1947
p: New Jersey

5 Celesta Durbin
b: Apr. 1880
d: Havre de Grace, MD
p:

6 George Washington Bond
b: Mar. 5, 1867
p: Peach bottom, Pennsylvania
m: Aug. 18, 1889
d: Jul. 9, 1944
p: St. James Gravel Hill

7 Amelia A. Harris
b: Nov. 28, 1872
p: Havre de Grace, MD
d: Jan. 12, 1947
p: St. James Gravel Hill

8 Jacob Bishop
b: 1848
p:
m:

9 Sarah Ushin
b: 1847
p: West Indies
d:
p:

10 Nathanial Durbin
b: Jul. 1860
m: Aug. 15, 1881

11 Hester Dennis
b: 1863
p:
p:

12 Wim. Harry Henry Bond
b: Feb. 28, 1805
p:
m:

13 Sarah A. E. Prigg
b: Apr. 1818
p:
p:

14 Lawson Harris
b: abt 1827
m: abt 1855
p:
p:

15 Margaret Hill
b: abt 1831
d:
p:

16 Isaac Bishop
d: abt 1888

17 Rachael Scott
b: abt 1811
d: Aug. 23, 1899

18

19
b:

20 Stephen Durbin
b: abt 1840
d: Nov. 22, 1908

21 Celesta A. Skinner
b: 1844
d:

22 Charles Dennis
b: 1836
d:

23 Susan
b: 1835
d:

24 Henry Bond
b: 1787
d:

25 Sophia
b:
d:

26 Mark Prigg
b: Feb. 21, 1891
p: Greenspring Cemetery, Level MD

27 Sarah Gilbert
b: 1782
d:

28 Hazzard Richard Harris
b: 1783
d: Apr. 9, 1876

29 Amelia Prigg
b: 1801
d: Aug. 1899

30 Russell Hill
b: 1795

31 Ruth
b: 1815
d:

32
33
34
35 Polly Barber
36
37
38
39
40 Bonaparte Durbin(m)
41 Grace Ramsey
42 Horace Skinner
43 Hatty Martin
44
45
46
47
48
49
50
51
52
53
54
55
56
57
b: 1790
58 Mark Prigg
59 Sarah Gilbert
60 Toney Hill
61
62
63

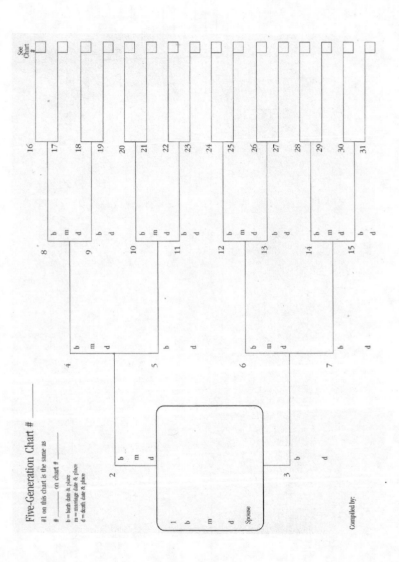

Five-Generation Chart # _____

#1 on this chart is the same as

_____ on chart # _____

b = birth date & place
m = marriage date & place
d = death date & place

Compiled by:

To schedule author Reginald M. Bishop for speaking engagements, please contact his agency at (866) 939-7355 or e-mail him at rmbkinship@gmail.com.